The Cambridge Introduction to
Mark Twain

Mark Twain is a central figure in nineteenth-century American literature, and his novels are among the best-known and most often studied texts in the field. This clear and incisive introduction provides a biography of the author and situates his works in the historical and cultural context of his times. Peter Messent gives accessible but penetrating readings of the best-known writings including *Tom Sawyer* and *Huckleberry Finn*. He pays particular attention to the way Twain's humour works and how it underpins his prose style. The final chapter provides up-to-date analysis of the recent critical reception of Twain's writing, and summarises the contentious and important debates about his literary and cultural position. The guide to further reading will help those who wish to extend their research and critical work on the author. This book will be of outstanding value to anyone coming to Twain for the first time.

PETER MESSENT is Professor of Modern American Literature at the University of Nottingham.

Cambridge Introductions to Literature

This series is designed to introduce students to key topics and authors. Accessible and lively, these introductions will also appeal to readers who want to broaden their understanding of the books and authors they enjoy.

- Ideal for students, teachers, and lecturers
- Concise, yet packed with essential information
- Key suggestions for further reading

Titles in this series:

The Cambridge Introduction to
Mark Twain

PETER MESSENT

CAMBRIDGE UNIVERSITY PRESS
Cambridge, New York, Melbourne, Madrid, Cape Town, Singapore, São Paulo

Cambridge University Press
The Edinburgh Building, Cambridge CB2 8RU, UK

Published in the United States of America by Cambridge University Press, New York

www.cambridge.org
Information on this title: www.cambridge.org/9780521670753

© Peter Messent 2007

First published 2007

Printed in the United Kingdom at the University Press, Cambridge

A catalogue record for this publication is available from the British Library

ISBN 978-0-521-85445-0 hardback
ISBN 978-0-521-67075-3 paperback

To Lou Budd, the best of Twain scholars, with thanks for his generosity and encouragement over the years.

Contents

Preface

Mark Twain is the most famous American writer of his period. He is known for his iconic appearance: as an elderly man in a white suit, with a mane of white hair, beetling eyebrows and a straggly moustache, with either cigar or billiard cue in hand. He is also remembered for his genius with the comic quip: 'We ought never to do wrong when people are looking', 'Man is the only animal that blushes. Or needs to.' But his writings are primarily responsible for his fame. *Adventures of Huckleberry Finn* stands at the foundations of an American vernacular literary tradition and his other best-known novels and travel-writings continue to be popular today.

The field of Twain biography and criticism is crowded, and his work and place in American literature continue to provoke argument and debate. *The Cambridge Introduction to Mark Twain* has been written to provide a starting guide to the author, his life, and some of his best works, and to reassess his reputation. Its intention is to present a clear and informative introduction that gives the reader a helpful entry point to the ongoing discussions his writings have provoked – many of them crucial to the field of American culture as a whole. The organisation of the book is straightforward. It starts with a brief outline of Twain's life and an overview of the historical and cultural context in which his writings can be placed. It then focuses on his main works – on Twain's humour, on his successful and influential early travel writings, and on his most successful and enduring novels: *The Adventures of Tom Sawyer* and *Adventures of Huckleberry Finn* and *A Connecticut Yankee in King Arthur's Court* and *Pudd'nhead Wilson.* These sections contain detailed analysis of the themes and narrative techniques of each text and key interpretative approaches to them. Other works are also briefly discussed in this section of the book. The final chapter provides analysis of the recent critical reception of Twain's work, with its contentious and important debates about his literary and cultural position. Reference is made, within this context, to his late texts. A final guide to further reading is aimed at those who wish to extend their research and critical work on the author.

This study comes from my own previous work on Twain and from the extensive critical heritage on which I draw. After a decade working primarily on Twain, I still thoroughly enjoy reading him and find him a fascinating figure in the way that his life and works provide a lens for the larger study of American life and culture in his own times and in our own. I will count this work successful if my own enthusiasm and interest stimulate the same response in my readers.

Note on referencing

Reference is made throughout this collection to the *Oxford Mark Twain*, the widely-available set of facsimiles of the first American editions of Mark Twain's works, edited by Shelley Fisher Fishkin and published by Oxford University Press in 1996. Where these editions are used, page referencing immediately follows the quotation given. In Chapter 2 (though not elsewhere), references to the stories published in *Mark Twain's Sketches, New and Old* (1875) are also to the Oxford edition. Similarly in Chapter 3, with *The Stolen White Elephant, Etc.* (1882). All other references to Twain's sketches, essays and short stories are to the two-volume edition of Twain's *Collected Tales, Sketches, Speeches, & Essays 1852–1890* (New York: Library of America, 1992). All such references are preceded in the text by the code *TSSE1* or *TSSE2* depending on the volume. A list of other primary texts follows. The letter codes that follow quotations are given in the final brackets.

Twain, Mark (1923). *Europe and Elsewhere.* New York: Harper. (*EE*)

Twain, Mark, and Howells, William Dean (1960). *Mark Twain-Howells Letters: The Correspondence of Samuel L. Clemens and William Dean Howells, 1872–1910*, 2 vols., ed. Henry Nash Smith and William M. Gibson. Cambridge, Mass.: Belknap. (*THL*)

Twain, Mark (1962). *Letters from the Earth*, ed. Bernard DeVoto. Greenwich, Conn.: Fawcett. (*LE*)

Twain, Mark (1969). *Mark Twain's Correspondence with Henry Huttleston Rogers. 1893–1909*, ed. Lewis Leary. Berkeley: University of California Press. (*TCR*)

Twain, Mark (1969). *The Mysterious Stranger*, ed. William M. Gibson. Berkeley: University of California Press. (*MS*)

Twain, Mark (1975). *Mark Twain's Notebooks & Journals, Vol. II (1877–1883)*, ed. Frederick Anderson, Lin Salamo and Bernard L. Stein. Berkeley: University of California Press. (*NJ2*)

Twain, Mark (1988). *Mark Twain's Letters. Volume 1. 1853–1866*, ed. Edgar Marquess Branch, Michael B. Frank and Kenneth M. Sanderson. Berkeley: University of California Press. (*L1*)

Twain, Mark (1990). *Mark Twain's Letters. Volume 2. 1867–1868*, ed. Harriet Elinor Smith and Richard Bucci. Berkeley: University of California Press. (*L2*)

Twain, Mark (1995). *Mark Twain's Letters. Volume 4. 1870–1871*, ed. Victor Fischer and Michael B. Frank. Berkeley: University of California Press. (*L4*)

Twain, Mark (1997). *Mark Twain's Letters. Volume 5. 1872–1873*, ed. Lin Salamo and Harriet Elinor Smith. Berkeley: University of California Press. (*L5*)

Chapter 1

Mark Twain's life

The early life

Samuel Langhorne Clemens (Mark Twain as he is better known) spent his early and formative years in Missouri, on what was then the south-western frontier. He lived first in the small village of Florida, then – from 1839, just before his fourth birthday – in the expanding river town of Hannibal. His father, John Marshall Clemens, was a businessman, property speculator, storekeeper and civic leader (justice of the peace and railroad promoter). His business ventures, though, were generally unsuccessful and he was, from his son's account, an emotionally reserved and stern man, whose Virginian ancestry gave him an exaggerated sense of his own dignity. He died, however, when Twain was still young, in 1847, of pneumonia after being caught in a sleet storm while returning from a neighbouring town.

Twain was much closer to his mother, Jane Lampton Clemens, and she was a key influence in his life. There must necessarily be a large hole in any attempt to trace the full pattern of the mother-son relationship. For, on the death in 1904 of Mollie Clemens, brother Orion's wife, Twain evidently asked that his letters to his mother – apparently 'almost four trunks' full – be destroyed (see *L5*, 728). We know, however, that Jane was warm, witty, outspoken, lively and – like her son – a good story-teller.

It was Jane who brought up the family (the four living children) after her husband's death and always under financial pressure. Her eldest son, Orion, ten years older than Twain, became the main wage-earner for the family, but his eccentricity, otherworldliness, and lack of business sense began a life-long series

1

of stumbles from one unsuccessful career to the next (Twain would support him financially for much of his later life). Twain himself started full-time work in 1848 or 1849 as an apprentice printer to Joseph Ament's *Missouri Courier*, and then (in January 1851) joined the newspaper Orion was now running (the *Hannibal Journal*) as printer and general assistant. These years were crucial to Twain's development, for his strong interest in the printing business would affect both his future business and literary careers. His experience as printer and compositor would also provide material for a major section in the late manuscript, *No. 44, The Mysterious Stranger*. His position also gave him a great deal of reading experience in different types of literature – widely reprinted at that time from one newspaper and journal to the next. It prompted him, in turn, to begin to write and publish a series of brief comic squibs and journalistic pieces of his own, mostly at a local level. But he was also published more widely: his earliest-known sketch to appear in the East, 'The Dandy Frightening the Squatter', appeared in the Boston *Carpet-Bag* on 1 May 1852.

Twain's time working for Orion was relatively short. Their different temperaments, Twain's awareness of the narrowness of his opportunities in Hannibal, as well (no doubt) as the sense of rapid economic expansion and movement in the boom economy of the 1850s, led him to leave the town in late May–June 1853. This was a move of huge importance, for he would return to Hannibal on only some seven occasions in his future life, and would – in Ron Powers' words – 'never live there again, never be a boy again, except in his literature and in his dreams.'[1]

Twain's Hannibal boyhood was crucial for the influence it had on the very best of his fiction. *Tom Sawyer, Huckleberry Finn, Pudd'nhead Wilson* and a series of other lesser-known texts are imaginatively located around that town and the life Twain lived there, the 'Matter of Hannibal'.[2] Many of Twain's own later memories of his early life are unreliable. And the picture many readers have of Hannibal as an idyllic and dream-like boyhood space is undoubtedly, in part, a product of the gap between the town's rural and pre-modern aspects and the post-Civil War, fast-modernising and urban-based America in which Twain later wrote and lived. But historical records do give us some reliable knowledge of that community.

It is now generally recognised that Twain's close boyhood contacts (through a slave economy) with African Americans, their speech and culture, had a powerful influence on him and his future writing. In Shelley Fisher Fishkin's words, 'black oral traditions and vernacular speech . . . played . . . an important role in shaping [his] art'.[3] But it has only recently become clear that the version of slavery Twain would have known in his boyhood Missouri (one based for the most part on small-scale ownership) was in some ways as demeaning and brutally violent as in the plantation economy of the deep South. Twain was himself directly affected by the presence of slavery in the town, for his father both traded in individual slaves and, as justice of the peace, enforced the Hannibal slave ordinance through public whippings. Terrell Dempsey recaptures in some detail the slave culture of the immediate region and 'the day-to-day, cradle-to-grave degradation experienced by the men, women, and children who made up one quarter of the population and labored for the other three quarters'[4]

Twain's own memories sometimes edited out the harsher aspects of local Hannibal slave-holding practice. But he became, as his life went on, a fierce opponent of what slavery as an institution meant. In some of his best work, he would depict the warping effect of slavery on both the Euro-Americans who condoned it and its African American victims, and would also undermine standard racial stereotyping. Such literary work can be traced inevitably back to the memories of his boyhood world. But this process was necessarily gradual. Living in a slave-holding society, Twain – when still young – undoubtedly shared its assumptions. This is clear in some of the letters following his June 1853 departure from Hannibal. Twain had gone to St Louis, where his sister Pamela lived. By late August, however, he was in New York, where he found work as a typesetter, reporting back to his family on urban life and on the city's World's Fair. In October he moved on to Philadelphia, then in February 1854 to Washington. His letters contain sharp descriptive detail and (with the later letters home from the West) form a type of apprentice work for his travel writing. But they also show evidence of his narrow-mindedness and bigotry at the time: 'I reckon I had better black my face, for in these Eastern States niggers are considerably better than white people' (*L1*, 4).

Twain's movements in this period can be seen as the start of a life-time pattern of often restless travelling, and also as the first spread of the wings of a lively-minded and adventurous young man. But unemployment followed, the letters dried up and Twain returned to his family (now moved), presumably for rest and recuperation. In January 1856, he was working in Keokuk, Iowa, alongside younger brother Henry in the Ben Franklin Book and Job Office – the business Orion had taken over following his marriage.

River boating, the Civil War, the West

The Mississippi River – Hannibal's main commercial artery – is a powerful geo-graphical and physical presence in Twain's work. Twain's fascination with the river and the role it plays in his literary and mythic imagination has been subject to considerable critical interest.[5] In *Life on the Mississippi*, Twain powerfully conjured up life in the 'white town' of his boyhood, 'drowsing in the sun-shine of a summer's morning', and how the cry from the 'negro drayman' of 'S-t-e-a-m-boat a'comin!' gave a centre to the day, had the 'dead town . . . alive and moving' (63–5). And his own apprenticeship and brief career as a steamboat pilot, romantically and famously recalled as 'the only unfettered and entirely independent human being that lived in the earth' (166), form the subject-matter of most of the early part of the book.

Twain had not stayed in Iowa long. More restless movement had followed, this time to Cincinnati and further printing work. Plans to travel to Brazil came to nothing. In April 1857 he boarded ship for New Orleans and fulfilled an old ambition by making an arrangement with the pilot, Horace Bixby, to become his steersman and apprentice (borrowing from a relative the considerable sum needed to seal this contract). Twain spent four years, first learning the river, then becoming a pilot himself. It was during this time, in June 1858, that his younger brother Henry – employed on the *Pennsylvania*, as a result of Twain's own efforts on his behalf – died as a result of the severe injuries he received when the boat's boilers exploded: a common occurrence on the river. Twain's grief and self-recrimination (for he was present while Henry was dying and was originally meant to be on the same boat) are clear in the moving letters he wrote at the time, and form part of a recurrent emotional pattern in his life.

Twain was a licensed pilot for just over two years. But in 1861, with the outbreak of the Civil War, Union forces blockaded the river and steamboat traffic was closed down. He then returned to Hannibal and was briefly (for two weeks only) involved with the Marion Rangers, a volunteer group with Confederate sympathies. Later, Twain would mine this incident in the short piece, 'The Private History of a Campaign That Failed', for its comic potential, but also to make serious anti-militaristic comment.

Twain would be conspicuously reticent about the Civil War in his writing career, but seems to have remained a Confederate sympathiser in the period immediately following his own brief part in it. Worried that he might be forced to act as a river pilot in the Union cause, he soon seized the opportunity to remove himself from the site of sectional conflict. So he accompanied Orion – who had managed to obtain the post of secretary of the Nevada Territory – out West. This was another highly significant period in Twain's life, to be imaginatively recreated (and comically distorted) in *Roughing It*. Twain started from St Louis for Nevada on 18 July 1861, intending to stay out West for three months. In fact, he was not to return East until 15 December 1866, when he set out by boat from San Francisco (via Nicaragua) to New York, to further his career there.

The time in the West was a crucial period in Twain's life, when, in his own words, he acknowledged his "'call" to literature, of a low order – *i.e.* humorous' (*L1*, 322). He worked a variety of jobs in Nevada. He was clerk in the legislature at Carson City and worked as a prospector and miner (during the gold and silver rush) in the Humboldt and Esmeralda districts. Finally – and most crucially – from September 1862 to March 1964 he became a newspaper reporter for the Virginia City *Territorial Enterprise*, and started using the pseudonym 'Mark Twain'. He then moved on to San Francisco, where he further established his literary identity, writing for newspapers and magazines and becoming a prominent member of the city's artistic community. Twain's life went through both high and low points in this last period (he was near-destitute at one stage and may even have considered suicide) and was punctuated by other activities. He spent two months in Tuolumne and Calaveras Counties (mining areas) from December 1864, and four months in Hawaii (18 March – 19 July 1866), contracted to write a series of travel letters. These two interludes had a greater effect on Twain's long-term career than their relative brevity might suggest. It was in the mining camps that he first heard the story that he rewrote as 'The Jumping Frog of Calaveras County', and which would first bring him nationwide fame. And it was on returning from Hawaii that he commenced his career as a humorous lecturer with 'Our Fellow Savages of the Sandwich Isles' – advertising his performance with the slogan, 'Doors open at 7 o'clock. The Trouble to begin at 8 o'clock'. He quickly gained a reputation in this role and would periodically return to the lecture platform throughout his life. Indeed, his celebrity, in part, depended on it.

Early success, marriage, the Hartford years

Once in New York, Twain quickly became a member of its Bohemian set. He published his first book, a compilation of some of his best sketches to date, *The Celebrated Jumping Frog of Calaveras County, and Other Sketches*, early in 1867. But his literary reputation was made with *The Innocents Abroad*. This best-selling travel book (and a lot more besides) both redefined the genre and caught the national pulse, reflecting a new mood of assertive American self-confidence following the end of the Civil War in 1865. Twain was originally contracted by the San Francisco *Alta California* – on the basis of his own enthusiasm for the venture – to send letters home from this 'pleasure excursion' (*L2*, 15), the voyage of the steamer *Quaker City* to Europe and the Holy Land (June – November, 1867). The letters were followed by their much expanded book-length version, written with the encouragement of the publisher, Elisha Bliss of

Hartford Connecticut. Bliss's American Publishing Company was a subscription company, its books sold in advance direct to the public by nationwide canvassers. Following the success of *Innocents*, Twain would stay with this firm for the next decade.

In late August 1868, Twain fell head-over-heels in love with Olivia Langdon, the sister of Charles ('Charley'), a fellow-traveller on the *Quaker City* trip. Olivia, the daughter of a wealthy businessman, would change the track of Twain's life. The social and moral environment of the Langdon Elmira home (Jervis, Olivia's father, was a committed abolitionist before the War) and the lively intellectual life there, helped play a major part in Twain's rise in status and respectability in the period.[6] He was now mixing in altogether more prestigious social circles and, counselled by Joseph Twichell, the Congregationalist minister and new friend he had met while visiting the wealthy and artistic Hartford community, Twain looked to meet Olivia's expectations and reform his previously bohemian lifestyle. With an (apparently genuine) new commitment to Christianity, he worked to modify his previous reputation as 'the Wild Humorist of the Pacific Slope', and to convince Olivia's parents that he could be a suitable match for their fragile and sensitive daughter. Against all the odds, he succeeded in this last aim.

Twain was honing his skills as a comic lecturer in this period, and boosted his finances with lecturing tours in the East and Midwest in 1868–69, and in New England in 1869–70. He married Olivia on 2 February 1870. Her father, Jervis, established Twain as co-owner and co-editor of the *Buffalo Express*, but the couple never really settled in that city and had to cope with a series of deaths (of Jervis, and Olivia's close friend, Emma Nye), and the poor health of their first child, Langdon (born 7 November 1870). Twain remained busy with the newspaper, lectures, business plans, even inventions, while working (and at first making slow progress) on *Roughing It*.

The move to Hartford in late 1871, though marred by the death of Langdon in June 1872, began the happiest period in Twain's married life. With the success of his early books and the financial support of Olivia, the couple were able to commission the building of the large house that was to serve as the family home from 1874–1891. During this Hartford period, his three daughters were born: Susy in 1872, Clara in 1874 and Jean in 1880.

The stability and friendships Twain found at a personal level in this community were matched by his professional success. However, much of his writing was done not in Hartford, but in the family's summer residence at Quarry Farm, Elmira (the home of Twain's sister-in-law Susan Crane). His first full-length work of fiction, *The Gilded Age* (1873), which gave a name to the political corruption and speculative economy of the times, was co-written with fellow

Hartford resident, Charles Dudley Warner. More travel books, *A Tramp Abroad* (1880) and *Life on the Mississippi* followed, but also the first group of Twain's most successful fictions, *The Adventures of Tom Sawyer* (1876), *The Prince and the Pauper* (1881) and *Adventures of Huckleberry Finn* (1885). The last book of real merit written in this period, *A Connecticut Yankee in King Arthur's Court* (1889), and particularly its dystopian ending, gives evidence of a darkening imaginative vision on the author's part, his bleaker view of human nature and of the process of history itself. But it is still a novel where many elements of his exuberant comic spirit remain intact.

In the early Hartford years, Twain's literary stock was on the rise. His friend, William Dean Howells, gave his books the most generous praise and also published his work in the prestigious literary magazine he edited, the *Atlantic Monthly*. Twain's response – torn as he always was between popular success and literary prestige and respectability – was to claim that 'the Atlantic audience . . . is the only [one] that I sit down before in perfect serenity (for the simple reason that it don't require a "humorist" to paint himself stripèd, & stand on his head every fifteen minutes.)' (*THL*, 49). But this was also the period in which the first signs of Twain's monetary problems started to surface. For he began (in true Gilded Age fashion) to extend himself on what would eventually prove to be too many fronts, establishing his own publishing company (Webster & Co.) in 1884, and sinking money into the development of the Paige Typesetting Machine, the invention that would prove his financial nemesis.

Expatriation, financial loss, family tragedy

Twain made many trips to Europe throughout his career usually with his family, sometimes to lecture, research, or to travel (preparing for his next book in that genre), sometimes just to save money from the expenses of the Hartford family life. But, from 1891–1900, Twain was virtually an expatriate, living most of the time in Europe, though frequently returning to the US. What began mainly as a money-saving exercise came to be more permanent, both because of the benefits to the family (Clara's training for a musical career and the treatment of Jean's epilepsy – first evidenced in 1890 but undiagnosed until 1896) and because of the catastrophic collapse of the family fortune. The drain of the typesetter investments, a general financial depression and a number of bad decisions on behalf of the Webster Company, meant that Twain's publishing business was forced into bankruptcy in 1894. His literary work dipped in quality, too, with *The American Claimant* (1892), though he would stage something of a recovery with his last major novel, *Pudd'nhead Wilson* (1894).

Howells remembered the period as the time when 'night was blackest' for Twain (*THL*, 649). The company's bankruptcy was a major blow and Twain himself took personal responsibility for the squaring of its debts. With the help of new friend, Henry H. Rogers, Vice-President of Standard Oil and, in the expression of the time, a 'robber baron', his finances were put on a firmer footing. And his 1895–96 round-the-world lecture tour (together with some astute financial manoeuvres by Rogers) enabled him to clear his debts by 1898. But in August 1896, following the tour, when Twain was staying just outside London and preparing to write *Following the Equator* (the book based on it), his eldest and best-loved daughter, Susy – who had remained in America during this period – unexpectedly died of spinal meningitis. This was a devastating blow for her parents, from which neither would fully recover. As Twain wrote to Rogers of this time: 'All the heart I had was in Susy's grave and the Webster debts' (*TCR*, 309).

Life however went on. Twain, almost always a prolific writer, plunged himself into his work and published fifteen books between 1889 (*Connecticut Yankee*) and 1900 (*The Man That Corrupted Hadleyburg and Other Stories and Essays*). In particular, the period spent by the family in Vienna from 1897–99 was marked by a surge of creativity. In 1900, they returned to New York to live in America but could no longer live in the Hartford house (and sold it) because of the memories it contained. In 1902, Olivia became seriously ill with heart problems. Twain moved the family to Italy in 1904 in search of a better climate for her health, but she died in June, causing further heartbreak for the family. For Twain himself this was a 'thunder-stroke' when, as he says, 'I lost the life of my life' (*TCR*, 569, 580).

The final years

By the last decades of Twain's life he was firmly established as a national and international celebrity and enjoying much of the attention this brought him. When living in New York, for instance, he would walk the Sunday streets in his famous white suit to coincide with the time the churches spilled their worshippers. During this period, he was more likely to speak in his own voice in his writing, giving his own opinions in a non-fiction mode, largely eschewing his comic persona. For example, he would eventually lend his significant public voice and presence to protest against the Philippine-American War of 1899–1902, and (more generally) against the larger combination of Christian missionary activity and western Imperialism.

Twain kept writing in his last decade, though much of it (like *No. 44, The Mysterious Stranger*) went unpublished at the time and he certainly let up somewhat after his seventieth birthday. But his pronouncements on public policy and historical events (as in *King Leopold's Soliloquy*, 1905) undoubtedly had their influence on his contemporaries. It was in these years that Twain spent much time on his *Autobiography*. He looked to re-invent the genre, using a method of free association and a mixture of material – letters, newspaper clippings, essays, present occurrences and past reminiscences. Bringing these together, he aimed to produce 'a form and method whereby the past and the present are constantly brought face to face, resulting in contrasts which newly fire up the interest all along, like contact of flint with steel'. And he operated what he called a 'deliberate system' of following a topic just as long as it interested him and then moving to another, 'the moment its interest for me is exhausted'.[7] This left him with a huge mass of material, much of it regarded by the author (because of its supposed controversial nature) as unpublishable in his own lifetime (much is still unpublished). One might see this as a Freudian talking cure that failed, a series of stories 'that eventually unraveled rather than affirmed the self'.[8] Or one can view it as an anticipatory form of 'postmodern' experimentation, a recognition that the self has no centre, and that any attempt to formally contain a life is an impossibility. It is, though, a text that has intrigued, and continues to intrigue, a later generation: five part-versions of it have already been published.

There are various conflicting accounts of Twain's final years. One of the most influential has been Hamlin Hill's, who in *Mark Twain: God's Fool* (1973) portrayed Twain as an unpredictably bad-tempered old man, vindictive, some-times worse-the-wear for drink and with a faltering memory. Estranged from his two remaining children, Twain's interest centred on his 'Angel Fish', the group of young girls he gathered around him in what Hill calls a 'more than avuncular' way. This 'Mark Twain', despairing and pessimistic, showed 'the geri-atric manifestations of a personality that had never been quite able to endure itself'.[9]

If there are elements of truth here, this is an over-harsh interpretation. The most recent biography of the later years, Karen Lystra's *Dangerous Intimacy* (2004) revises this account to show an artist and a man who was still able to enjoy life and to write memorably, one who cannot be confined to a single dimension: 'a person of many moods, in and out of print – gloomy and pessimistic but also cheerful, energetic, and loving'. Lystra reads the 'Angel Fish' in terms of the 'compensatory gesture', Twain seeking to fill 'a deep emotional hole' with these 'surrogate children'. For the young girls may have reminded him of the dead

Susy, perhaps recalled 'his own lost youth', or fed 'some lifelong nostalgia for the honesty and simplicity of childhood'.[10]

The author's relationship with his own two daughters was, however, problematic in this period. In the story as Lystra tells it, this was largely caused by the influence of Twain's secretary and housekeeper, Isabel Lyon – a schemer whose 'most treasured goal [was] to walk down the aisle with America's greatest literary celebrity'.[11] The epileptic Jean was more or less banished from her father's house, while Clara, looking to establish a separate identity outside her father's powerful scan, took little part in the emotional life of the household, pursuing her career and separate life, often distancing herself physically from her father's presence.

This whole scenario – and Twain's later banishing of Lyon and her husband, his business advisor Ralph Ashcroft – smacks somewhat of melodrama (lonely and confused old and famous writer controlled by manipulative spinster gold-digger). And it is likely a more balanced version of this undoubtedly complicated story remains to be told – for a reading of Lyon's diary suggests her good faith, that she may have been as much sinned against as sinning. Undoubtedly Twain was very lonely at times in his last years, living in 'Stormfield', the house near Redding, Connecticut, which John Howells (William Dean Howells's son) had designed for him. Undoubtedly too, his relationship with his daughters was difficult and Jean in particular suffered from his neglect. Twain evidently realised this and felt considerable guilt for it, finally bringing her back to Stormfield to live with him, to act as his secretary and housekeeper. But on Christmas Eve, 1909, Jean was found dead in her bath after an epilepsy attack. Twain's telegram message to well-wishers was 'I thank you most sincerely, but nothing can help me'.[12] And on 21 April 1910, he too would die – a victim of the heart trouble that had plagued him in his final year.

Chapter 2

Contexts

Samuel Langhorne Clemens and 'Mark Twain' *17*

Samuel Clemens (Mark Twain) was born on 30 November 1835. The siege of the Alamo began some three months later, on 23 February 1836, with the subsequent declaration of Texan independence from Mexico by American settlers on 2 March. On 25 February 1836, New England inventor Samuel Colt patented the first revolver. At the end of the century, Twain would become a spokesman against American imperialism and a critic of the violence that accompanied it. And in *A Connecticut Yankee in King Arthur's Court* he would create a protagonist, Hank Morgan, who 'learned [his] real trade' at Samuel Colt's 'great arms factory' in Hartford, Connecticut: 'learned to make everything; guns, revolvers, cannon, boilers, engines, all sorts of labor-saving machinery' (20). Irony would always be a primary tool in Twain's own comic artillery (for humour, as he would explicitly comment, carries its own weaponry) and it sounds strongly in that last phrase.

On the one hand, there seems no connection between Twain's birth and these historical events. On the other, this is one in a number of quirky coincidences and near-coincidences that feature in Twain's life, (unknowingly) predictive of significant concerns and paradoxes in his subsequent career. Twain was, and remains, an iconic figure in the American popular imagination. Yet he conducted an ongoing – if often disguised – quarrel with his country and its dominant value-system. And conflicts over territory, definitions of national and regional identity, the use of (various types of) violence, and the intersection of such violence with issues of race and gender – all subjects in some way touched on above – are issues he recurrently explored.

In her short essay on Twain's now best-known novel, *Adventures of Huckleberry Finn*, Toni Morrison judges it an 'amazing, troubling book'. Praising it for a 'language cut for its renegade tongue and sharp intelligence,' she calls it a work of 'classic literature, which is to say it heaves, manifests and lasts'.[1] We might extend this verdict beyond the limits of this single work. One distinctive quality of Twain's writings comes from his role as a comic writer: his need

11

to entertain a mass audience even as he might critique its most deeply-held assumptions. His work heaves and lasts as it has continued to speak to each different generation of readers, address their own contemporary concerns and interrogate their values. Though I am uncomfortable with Morrison's phrase 'classic literature' (and return to this issue in my final chapter), I nonetheless agree with the spirit of her remark. In this book, I look to show how Twain's best work – as we now judge it – continues to engage the needs and concerns of our early-twenty-first-century age.

To explore Twain's work through a historical lens is to notice the different ways his writing has been read and received over time and the varying popularity of its individual parts. In his lifetime, Twain was initially best-known for his travel writing (a generic label necessarily restrictive given his stretching of the boundaries of the form). *Innocents Abroad* was an immediate best-seller, with 69,156 copies of the American edition sold during its first year, and 125,479 copies – a massive number for its time – sold by 1879. *Roughing It*, Twain's account of the American West, was not far behind with 96,083 copies sold by 1879. In comparison, his novels were less immediately successful. Twain's publisher sold only 23,638 copies of *The Adventures of Tom Sawyer* in its first year – though there were a large number of pirated copies sold – and just 28,959 by the end of 1879. Over Twain's lifetime, however, this novel ended up outselling all his other books. *Adventures of Huckleberry Finn* had much better early sales, some 39,000 copies during its first month. And it has now, of course, become perhaps the most celebrated and best-known novel in American literary history, exceeding twenty million sales world-wide by the 1990s.[2]

But like all novels, Twain's most famous book is not what we might call a stable text. For its reception and interpretation has altered according to its different historical audiences and the critical communities they have formed. When *Huckleberry Finn* first came out, reviewers did not see it as a novel about race, but rather focused on its representation of juvenile 'delinquency', on Huck's position outside the boundaries of conventional respectability.[3] It was this that caused the Concord Library Committee to denounce the book and ban it from its shelves as 'trash and suitable only for the slums'. Twain's response was typical, seeing this as 'a rattling tip-top puff which will go into every paper in the country ... [and] sell 25,000 copies for us sure' (*THL*, 524–5). Readings of the novel that focused on its racial theme came much later. And critics have only relatively recently started to turn from the pre-Civil War setting of the book to interpret its final section in terms of the post-bellum period in which Twain was writing. Jim's manipulation by Tom in the final (evasion) sequence is accordingly seen as a veiled critique of the second-class status of

African Americans in the South in the 1880s, overwhelmingly subject to the whims and wishes of white 'mastery'.

The way in which Twain's books continue to release new meanings for each generation of readers also helps to explain the changing reputations of his texts. Thus *Pudd'nhead Wilson*, for instance, has had considerable attention in a recent period when racial issues and anxieties about personal identity and agency – twinned subjects in this novel about twin-ship – are both high on the critical and social agenda. So, too, with *The Adventures of Tom Sawyer*. The novel has usually been seen as reflecting a nostalgic desire for a simpler and earlier way of life increasingly distant from the urban and technological developments of Gilded Age America. Undoubtedly, such a reading was a primary factor in the book's success in Twain's lifetime. This approach has been complicated by recent interest in the construction of whiteness in American national identity. Accordingly, the novel – remembered most often and significantly for its whitewashing scene – has now been re-visioned, with attention paid to the conspicuous and almost complete absence of slavery in the book, and to the way Indian Joe plays out the role of a feared racial 'other'. I return to all these interpretative issues later.

Readers, then, have valued and responded to Twain's works differently as times have changed. So, the foreign policy of the Bush administration helps to account for the present upsurge of interest in his anti-imperialist late writing. When Kurt Vonnegut Jr, in many ways the present day inheritor of Twain's satiric mantle, speaks scornfully of 'our great victory over Iraq', it is Twain he first recalls: 'One of the most humiliated and heartbroken pieces Twain ever wrote [was] . . . about the slaughter of 600 Moro men, women and children by our soldiers during our liberation of the people of the Philippines after the Spanish-American War'.[4] Not everyone will agree that recent American intervention in Iraq can be read in relation to Twain's comments on earlier American military interventions and 'missionary' activities. But for many, his work continues to function as a significant sounding-board for our twenty-first century concerns.

Twain's writings, though, can be read in curiously conflicted ways. Thus *A Connecticut Yankee in King Arthur's Court* has been interpreted as both a hymn to American technological progress and a warning against its disastrous results. *Tom Sawyer* works both as an exercise in nostalgia, as a (silent) reminder of a society built on the foundations of slavery and as an indicator of the entrepreneurial values necessary to succeed in a post-Civil War competitive and capitalist age. Twain's fiction looks backward and forward, and taps a peculiar reservoir of both pleasure and confidence anxiety on the larger cultural level. Its mixture of comedy and of brooding doubt (which is often at least partly concealed) helps to account for its power and popularity in its own time, and since.

But Twain's work also gives us a window on American history in a crucial time of change. We might remember Henry Adams (Twain's junior, but whose life and career overlapped) 'pondering on the needs of the twentieth century', and looking back on his own boyhood from a half-century-later vantage point, to comment that: '[I]n essentials like religion, ethics, philosophy; in history, literature, art; in the concepts of all science, except perhaps mathematics, the American boy of 1854 stood nearer the year 1 than to the year 1900'.[5] Twain's fiction and non-fiction reflect something of this massive sense of change. For they take the reader from the pre-modern antebellum south-western small-town settlements of *Tom Sawyer, Huckleberry Finn* and *Pudd'nhead Wilson* through to the booming and expansionist modernised America of the post-war period, and to the turn-of-the-century imperialist adventures later built on such foundations.

The Civil War was a landmark event in this transition, one of the major watersheds in American history. Perhaps because of Twain's own southern background, this event forms a significant lacuna in his representation of the national scene and is only briefly touched on in his work. In *Roughing It*, Twain describes the far-western American frontier in, and immediately following, the wartime period, but the war itself is hardly mentioned. The silver-mining rush provides the historical centre of the book, though he is also concerned with the (accompanying) growth of industrial capitalism and its incorporating practices and the challenge this posed to standard American expectations of unfettered selfhood. The same is largely true in *Life on the Mississippi*, a history of the river that pivots around the Civil War in its focus both on the 'heyday of the steamboating prosperity' (41) and its consequent decline, as modes of transportation and commercial practice changed. The War, which coincided with, and helped to cause this decline is discussed in the book, but usually in passing. By 1882, when Twain returned to the river, he found only 'a wide and soundless vacancy, where the serried hosts of commerce used to contend' (255). Twain misses the bustling and romantic steamboat era even as, paradoxically, he celebrates the massive industrial progress of the post-war years.

Twain, then, does directly address American historical change in his work especially in his travel books, even if his treatment of it is selective. In his fiction, however, his engagement with the major issues of his time is more oblique and his attitude toward them often ambiguous. There are, however, exceptions to this rule. *The Gilded Age: A Tale of To-Day* was Twain's first attempt at a novel, co-written with his neighbour and friend, Charles Dudley Warner. Here, the two men produced a sprawling narrative describing the frenzied speculative activity and corrupt political and legal behaviour of the time, thus naming the whole historical period. But the novel is far from being a poker-faced representation of such excess. Rather, it works both as satire and – at least in part – as broad comedy, through Twain's invention of the figure of Colonel Beriah Sellers. Sellers is a man of endless optimism and inevitable failures, seen as at his most typical as he welcomes Washington Hawkins – the novel's early main protagonist – to a family dinner consisting only of an 'abundance of clear, fresh water, and a basin of raw turnips', meanwhile he piles up 'several [imaginary] future fortunes' as he chatters of the business schemes in which he is engaged (109–12). His countless 'get-rich-quick' schemes are only matched by the hyperbolic intensity of his language. Unsurprisingly, given Twain's own taste for inventions, speculative propensities and money-making ventures, Sellers would remain a favourite character, reappearing in both stage and novel form.

Twain would return to Washington life and to an updated depiction of contemporary American social conditions in *The American Claimant* (1892). However, the concern with immediate historical events is less strongly evident here, as Sellers (now renamed 'Mulberry') and his various imaginative schemes move even more centre stage. The most fantastically extravagant of these is the scheme for the scientific 'materialization' (or re-animation) of dead men to use as policemen, soldiers and the like – a plan with, in Sellers's words, 'billions in it – billions' (46).

What I am suggesting here is that even in the fictions where Twain does represent his own historical period, there is always something that works against what we would call a realist mode. Realism is a term that denotes the representation of everyday conditions in an apparently transparent manner – the objective and straightforward description of the social and historical world which author and audience see before them. In *The American Claimant*, Twain's portrayal of one of his main protagonists, Howard Tracy, as – for instance – he attends a Mechanics Debating Society in Washington, or describes the routines of his boarding-house world, does not stray all that far from this model. But the other aspects of the novel – Sellers's larger-than-life and often ludicrous character and the comic absurdity and fantastic nature of the materialisation motif, for example – certainly take us a long way from the genre.

Realism is a more problematic and interesting term than my definition above suggests and I will return to the subject later in the book. In the majority of his fictions, though, – and certainly in those that are best-known – Twain moves away from any direct engagement with his post-Civil War American world. That world remains, however, *indirectly* very much at the centre of his attentions, its history represented in disguised or less-than-straightforward ways.

So, for example, he turns any notion of 'everyday reality' upside down in *A Connecticut Yankee*, by the introduction of an obviously *unreal* scenario: a fantasy version of a sixth-century Arthurian world to set against Hank Morgan (and the author's own) contemporary America. He still, nonetheless, addresses the concerns and conditions of that later time. The novel can be read as a critique of scientific knowledge, of the value Americans placed on technological efficiency and various forms of rationalisation, and of the very assumptions made about the relationship between history and progress in the late nineteenth-century western world.

One of my main intentions in the chapter that follows is to suggest the misleading nature of the apparent simplicity of many of Twain's narratives and how difficult they can be to interpret in an obvious and one-dimensional way. Many of his novels are set outside his own period – the three Mississippi novels (*Tom Sawyer, Huckleberry Finn* and *Pudd'nhead Wilson*) are set before the Civil War. He moves from one genre to another, writing in *Connecticut Yankee* a book which is both fantasy and historical romance and in *Pudd'nhead Wilson* one that moves between determinist fable and a type of detective story. He even shifts completely away from an American geographical base in *Connecticut Yankee*, the *Mysterious Stranger* manuscripts, and other fictional texts. In all these cases, however, he addresses themes and issues of vital relevance to his own time: the impact of modernisation and what it meant to previous ideas of human agency (the authority to control and direct one's own fate); the changing racial landscape and the problems associated with it; anxieties about business values and masculinity in an era of capitalist expansion. These are just a few of the key concerns that underlie – and trouble – his fictional world.

It is difficult to say how conscious Twain was of the social relevance of his fiction. His moves away from realism may suggest that he did not intend to engage with troubling contemporary issues, but that they could not help but enter his fiction in some form. Or they could indicate that, as a humorist who depended on the allegiance of a popular audience, he knew that any contentious social concerns were best approached in an indirect way, masked by the comedy expected of him. The truth probably lies somewhere in between the two scenarios. Such indirection, however, does give a certain ambiguity and interpretative instability to his texts. This may be an inevitable by-product of the relationship between the literary forms he used, the comedy that drove them and the more serious content they in fact, contained. Or it may be the result of tensions and paradoxes within his own values and beliefs. In the chapter that follows, I unpack some of the ways we can read the fiction, expose some of its various ambiguities and look to connect it to its late-Victorian American context. Any work of this type is bound to be partial and to do other and different critical approaches less than full justice. The guide to further reading at the end of this book will provide a framework allowing some of those gaps to be filled.

Samuel Langhorne Clemens and 'Mark Twain'

Any introduction to the context within which we read Clemens's works must explain and explore the use of the 'Mark Twain' persona within them. Immediately, though, I run into difficulties with the use of the Clemens/Twain name. For the majority of this book I refer to the author as Mark Twain for ease and convenience (Joseph Twichell, one of his closest friends, always called him 'Mark'). But sometimes, as here, I distinguish between the author (Clemens) and his nom de plume. At other points I need to show how the use of 'Mark Twain' as a protagonist in the texts differs from Mark Twain as an authorial identity. I trust such differences – and the need to draw lines between them – will become clear as I continue.

Clemens's use of a nom de plume and construction of an alternative persona merely copies what was standard procedure for comic writers in mid-nineteenth-century America. After the early use of other pseudonyms, Clemens began writing under the name 'Mark Twain' (a riverboat warning for shallow, and thus dangerous water of two 'marks' or fathoms) out West, in the Nevada Territory, in 1863. This name did not just refer to the assumed identity of the author. For the common use of a first-person voice made 'Mark Twain' the (usually) comic *subject* of the sketches and travel writings – a comically distorted or invented version of the authorial self – as well as their teller. The authorial name Mark Twain, though, could often be used (particularly in the later years) in a deadly serious way. When Twain wrote on Imperialism and on war under this soubriquet, the opinions he gave were clearly his own. However, when he wrote about his own direct autobiographical past (in the *Autobiography*, in reminiscences and elsewhere) to tell the story of Samuel Clemens's own past life, the facts he gives are often deeply unreliable. Thus a complicated interchange takes place between at least five identities – Samuel Clemens the man, the Samuel Clemens whose history is recovered in Twain's work, Mark Twain the author, the persona 'Mark Twain', a semi-fictional protagonist who plays the leading part in so many sketches and travel books and the Mark Twain who speaks in the first-person voice or appears within the author's work, but who (in this case) directly represents that author.

I return to this important subject in Chapter 3 and, as I do so, will further clarify some of the above distinctions. Here, though, I briefly indicate a few of the shapes taken by the 'Mark Twain' persona, using the early collection, *Mark Twain's Sketches: Old and New* (1875), to do so. This book was put together when the author was still refining his technique and was using less restrained and more various versions of his first-person protagonist and reporter than would later be the case. In 'How I Edited an Agricultural Paper', 'Mark Twain' initially presents himself as an inexperienced and shallow-headed replacement newspaper editor who startles his readers with the wild inaccuracies of his reporting. So, for instance, he recommends 'the domestication of the pole-cat on account of its playfulness and its excellence as a ratter' (237) and tells of the coming of warm weather as 'the ganders begin to spawn' (235).

But this 'Mark Twain' then turns out to be a fake and deliberately foolish version of the first-person protagonist and speaker. For when the returning permanent editor of the paper criticises his actions, the 'real', and more astute, 'Twain'[6] turns the tables on him by revealing his real journalistic motives and experience. He also reveals the satiric sensibility of which (as it unexpectedly turns out) he is capable. The narrative movement of the sketch completely changes direction as the editor challenges the narrator on his lack of knowledge of his subject (agriculture). 'Twain' replies by pointing to his success in stimulating the interest of his readers. Claiming that 'the less a man knows the bigger the noise he makes and the higher the salary he commands' (238), he cites drama criticism, book reviewing and financial reporting as evidence of the general ignorance of the press in these (and other) areas. The sketch thus ends as a satiric commentary on journalism and its general reliance on the substitution of imaginative fictions for factual knowledge – a sign of a slap-dash approach but also normal tactics used to boost readership numbers.

But the satire works in more than one way. For we, as readers of this sketch, have been 'hooked' (like his paper's readers) by the imaginative fictions 'Twain' has practised as agricultural editor. So we too, like the real editor, have our expectations turned upside down when his real status and motives are revealed. Unlike the agricultural newspaper's audience, we read his original journalism – within the context of this sketch – as both comedy and fiction. Nonetheless, in throwing our initial interpretation of his own character into disarray, Twain throws a spanner into our own assumptions of readerly intelligence and superiority – just gives a warning of our own tendencies to take the exaggerations we may read for the truth.

My unpicking of the way Twain constructs more than one persona in this sketch, and of the way his humour and his satire work, is long-winded and clumsy compared to the economy of the sketch itself. But this is part of my point. Twain's use of persona may appear simple. In fact, though, his art is skilled and never quite as obvious as it seems. My main ongoing point here, though, is to suggest something of the range of personae Twain adopts in his early work. The first version of 'Mark Twain' we are given (as an ignorant agricultural journalist) obviously relies on comic exaggeration, but it cannot be completely divorced from biography – the various newspaper work Twain had done in his youth and the comic mischief he had sometimes wrought in this role. So in many of these early sketches, Twain moves between humorous and hyperbolic versions of his own life experiences and complete comic invention to achieve his effects – with the reader not quite knowing where on this spectrum any such representation lies.

'My Watch', the first sketch in the book, centres on the protagonist's frustration with a faulty watch and the failed repairs carried out on it. The sketch – and the narrator's frustration – climax as the final watch-maker consulted speaks in a manner which seems surreal, but is in fact explained by his previous career as a steamboat engineer: 'She makes too much steam – you want to hang the monkey-wrench on the safety-valve!' Comic violence then follows, with the irritated 'Mark Twain' as its perpetrator: 'I brained him on the spot, and had him buried at my own expense' (20). In 'To Raise Poultry', the persona assumed is that of rapscallion and petty thief as Twain plays on the pun in the sketch title:

> I may say without egotism that as early as the age of seventeen I was acquainted with all the best and speediest ways of raising chickens, from raising them off a roost by burning lucifer matches under their noses, down to lifting them off a fence on a frosty night by insinuating the end of a warm board under their heels.   (81)

In other sketches, however, like 'Disgraceful Persecution of a Boy', the authorial Mark Twain comes to figure far more centrally, as a first-person voice lacking the kind of comic masks I have thus far illustrated. The barbed and ironic comments made here on the lack of 'rights' for the Chinese in San Francisco and on the emptiness of America's official rhetoric (as 'an asylum for the poor and the oppressed of all nations', 118–19) clearly come straight from the writer and are meant to have a political and social effect on his audience.

I have given a brief glimpse of the instability and variety of the Twain persona here and of the sometimes complex relationship between the authorial voice and the first-person protagonist he gives us. Twain's early sketches show him trying out the multiple uses of this persona. In *Innocents Abroad*, his first full-length book that is also a sustained narrative, the 'Mark Twain' protagonist becomes more centred and coherent, a figure capable of carrying and shaping an entire text. This is not to say that he does not appear in various and different guises: he does (as my later section on the book in Chapter 3 shows). But the one main narrator, at some points acting as a straightforward stand-in for the author and, at others, clearly a fictional and comic version of him, can contain such moves. Twain is still finding his direction here, but his use of the first-person voice within this book is as significant in its own way as that of the other first-person voice in his best (and best-known) novel, *Huckleberry Finn*.

The various uses of the 'Mark Twain' persona are crucial to any understanding of the author's work. Twain is a writer whose repertoire often depends on autobiographical material, so any reader needs constantly to negotiate between what he or she knows of his actual life and personality and the various versions of the persona that thread their way through the writing. 'Mark Twain' is always, in some way, related to the authorial self and the story of Samuel Clemens/Mark Twain's life is contained in large part – sometimes in wildly exaggerated and distorted form, sometimes not – in the narratives that he writes. *Roughing It* tells of the early 1860s, the years Twain spent in the far West. *Life on the Mississippi* is, in part, the story of his years as a river pilot (1857–1861). But, because Clemens is constructing an often-comic version of himself, any accurate and objective version of his life remains in suspension as we read the books.

In *Innocents Abroad*, Twain does occasionally point us in the direction of his own earlier life. So, for instance, the recounting of a traumatic childhood incident follows his description of a disturbing sculpture he has been shown in Milan cathedral – that of a 'man without skin; with every vein, artery, muscle, every fibre and tendon and tissue of the human frame, represented in minute detail'. He discusses the 'fascination' of this 'hideous thing', and the way that he foresees it entering and disturbing his future dreams. Twain undoubtedly possessed (rather like Huck Finn) a morbid and nightmarish quality to his imagination. This emerges clearly here, when he talks of the nature of these imagined dreams: 'I shall dream that it is stretched between the sheets with me and touching me with its exposed muscles and its stringy cold legs' (175).[7]

But it is the switch from present occurrence (and its future ramifications) to past event that is my main interest here. One of the things that makes Twain's travel books so distinctive is his way of following chains of mental association that disrupt the chronology and apparent narrative logic of his text. So here, the matter at hand triggers a memory of past boyhood time. Twain recalls an occasion when he played truant from school before, late at night, climbing in his father's office window to sleep in that room, out of 'a delicacy about going home and getting thrashed.' Lying on a lounge, and getting used to the darkness, Twain remembers how 'I fancied I could see a long, dusky, shapeless thing stretched upon the floor.' As the boy suffers cold shivers and trembles, with 'an awful sinking at the heart,' the naked upper-body of a corpse, a stab-wound in its breast, is gradually revealed. The boy runs home, receives his whipping with some delight (given the much greater shock to his system that he has just endured) and discovers that the body is that of a man stabbed nearby earlier that day and carried to his father's office for (unsuccessful) doctoring. Twain then ends the sequence with the words: 'I have slept in the same room with him often, since then – in my dreams' (175–7).

A similar type of passage occurs in Twain's last travel book *Following the Equator* (1897). In Bombay he sees a 'burly German' give 'a brisk cuff on the jaw' to a native servant. This act takes him straight back to his own south-western boyhood (and to the slavery that was an accepted part of that time and region), for there 'flashed upon me the forgotten fact that this was the *usual* way of explaining one's desires to a slave'. He then remembers his father's occasional cuffings of 'our harmless slave boy, Lewis, for trifling little blunders and awkwardnesses'. More disturbingly, he recalls, 'when I was ten years old [seeing] a man fling a lump of iron-ore at a slave-man in anger, for merely doing something awkwardly ... It bounded from the man's skull, and the man fell and never spoke again. He was dead in an hour' (351–2). Twain draws attention to the power of memory and its capacity to bridge both time and space so dramatically – 'Back to boyhood – fifty years; back to age again, another fifty; and a flight equal to the circumference of the globe – all in two seconds by the watch!' (352).

These are powerful and significant autobiographical passages. Both sequences provide textual signs (two among many) of the way that death and violence recurrently play on Twain's writerly imagination. The second suggests how the subject of race haunts much of his late writing.[8] Both passages are indicative of trauma. For a ten-year-old boy to see such violent and sudden deaths, whatever the social and historical context, would have a long-lasting emotional effect. The ready recollection of the slavery memory, some half a century later, suggests as much.

The more one reads of Twain as he re-writes his own life, however, the more one realises the dangers of placing too great a reliance on the factual accuracy of such reports. This is not to say that such incidents as the above were not based on fact. It is though, to recognise that Twain, in Ron Powers's words, had a 'mythifying imagination' and exercised 'a kind of psychic editing' over autobiographical materials: 'he was forever revising his life to make it even more interesting and melodramatic than it had been'.[9] The lesson here is clear: whatever Twain says in his writings (including the vast series of texts that compose his *Autobiography*) must be received with care. We can take his stories about his past as a partial representation of the biographical 'truth' but that is as far as we should go.

Chapter 3

Works

Twain's humour

Twain's phenomenal success as a writer came first and foremost because he was very funny. His particular background (and especially his time in the West) and the antidote he provided to the more genteel forms of comedy of the time, go some way towards explaining his impact. So too does his avoidance of the phonetic techniques of many of the fellow humorists with whom he had most in common. For example, Artemus Ward begins his 'The Press' with the sentence: 'I want the editers to cum to my Show free as the flours of May, but I don't want um to ride a free hoss to deth.'[1] And Twain's quick-witted responses to day-to-day events and his apparent ability to produce a comic quip at will were legendary. His May 1897 reply to a London newspaper correspondent following rumours of his demise, 'the report of my death was an exaggeration' – or, as it has been refined in folk memory, 'the reports of my death have been greatly exaggerated' – is now part of our cultural repertoire of best-known quotations. While some of his ironic aphorisms from 'Pudd'nhead Wilson's Calendar' (in *Pudd'nhead Wilson*) are also well-known:

> *October* 12, *the Discovery*. It was wonderful to find America, but it would have been more wonderful to miss it.   (301)

> Training is everything. The peach was once a bitter almond; cauliflower is nothing but cabbage with a college education.   (67)

'Pudd'nhead Wilson's New Calendar,' in *Following the Equator*, too, contains its own sharp ironies and aphorisms: 'The very ink with which all history is written is merely fluid prejudice' (699).

To try and define Twain's humour, especially in a short chapter section, is over-ambitious. To analyse humour, anyway – as many commentators have noted – is to risk bringing it crashing to the ground with leaden explanation. As E. B. White wrote: 'Humor can be dissected as a frog can, but the thing dies in the process and the innards are discouraging to any but the pure scientific mind.'[2] Twain's own best known short work, the sketch that brought him instant celebrity, 'The Celebrated Jumping Frog of Calaveras County' cannot help but spring to mind with this metaphor. I give some brief idea of the way that Twain's humour works, working in a highly selective manner and trawling through his writing career. But I hope that my explanations do not overly weigh that humour down, and thereby allow Twain's metaphorical frogs to keep on jumping.

Twain's humour takes many forms and it is this that helps, in part, to account for his massive success. He was particularly well-known in his early newspaper career for his hoaxes: the taking-in of his readers with the poker-faced telling of outrageous stories that at first glance appear to be true, but with the kind of exaggerated or pointed detail that indicates their actual unreliability. 'A Bloody Massacre Near Carson' (1863) is a very short piece with – significantly (for Twain's humour would often have a serious intent at its core) – a sober point to make, in its protest against the fraudulent inflation of dividends in the Nevada mining business. The main business of the sketch, though, lies in its description of a 'bloody massacre' committed near Carson City by a man called Hopkins, known to be 'subject to fits of violence'. Twain recounts how:

> About ten o'clock on Monday evening Hopkins dashed into Carson, on horse-back, with his throat cut from ear to ear, and bearing in his hand a reeking scalp [later found to be his wife's] from which the warm, smoking blood was still dripping, and fell in a dying condition in front of the Magnolia saloon.

Detail is then piled on bloody detail as the bodies of six of Hopkins's nine children are found with 'their brains . . . evidently . . . dashed out with a club' (*TSSE1*, 57). An explanation for the man's actions is then given: the loss of his savings due to stock-market fraud. If the description of Hopkins's original condition (riding into town with his 'throat cut from ear to ear') and the dramatic extremes of violence in the account suggest its fictional quality, many readers evidently were completely taken in by the hoax. This type of humour would be one that continued to attract Twain's literary attention. It operates around the narrow dividing line that can sometimes separate the literal truth and what is unbelievable. It tends to ask questions, too, about the status and reliability of our knowledge of the world in which we live – what we can trust (in this case a newspaper report) and how we can know we can trust it?

Twain was also fond of burlesque – the imitating and exaggeration of ways of speaking or behaving or of literary styles for the purposes of ridicule. He took as his particular target those romantic or sentimental forms that his own much tougher (and more modern) aesthetic looked to undermine and replace. So, for example, he creates comedy at the expense of a naive racial romanticism in 'A Day at Niagara' (1869). Approaching 'a gentle daughter of the aborigines' on a visit to the Falls, 'Mark Twain' addresses her: 'Is the heart of the forest maiden heavy? Is the Laughing-Tadpole lonely? Does she mourn over the extinguished council-fires of her race . . . ?' Inevitably the comic pay-off comes, here in the humour of ethnic stereotype, when the supposed Indian maiden opens her mouth: 'Faix, an is it Biddy Malone ye dare to be callin' names! Lave this or I'll shy your lean carcass over the catharact, ye sniveling blagyard!' (*TSSE1*, 303).

Twain uses an enormous variety of comic techniques early in his career: satire, the venting of a mock-abusive spleen, wild exaggeration and the clash of different types of languages, behaviours and patterns of comprehension. He was particularly fond of the use of digression – where the readers' expectations are frustrated as the controlling textual voice leads them off in unexpected and deliberately pointless narrative directions. His humour also relies on the gap between the controlling authorial position and the representation of the character and voice of the 'Mark Twain' protagonist and on the playfulness of the relationship between language and the reality it describes. These (and many others) are all techniques that Twain refines and develops – and sometimes abandons – as his career develops and as his control over his comic materials becomes increasingly skilful. To suggest just something of Twain's comic ability, I focus briefly on his first great success, the 'Jumping Frog' sketch, before offering a highly selective overview of his humorous career, illustrating as I do so something of its increasingly darkening tone.

The 1865 publication date of 'Jim Smiley and his Jumping Frog' is of considerable significance. For this was the year the American Civil War ended. Contemporary delight in Twain's sketch can, in part, be explained by the fact that the legacy of Northern and Southern animosity could temporarily be put aside in the shared enjoyment of a comic sketch set in the West (a geographical space beyond the arena of the fighting and removed from the main impact of sectional conflict), written by an adopted westerner, and in a distinctively

'American' literary style. The 'courtly muses' of Europe, which Ralph Waldo Emerson asked his countrymen to reject, could not be cast further aside than in this story. For the setting is an 'old dilapidated tavern in the ancient mining camp of Boomerang', and the dominant narrative voice – which belongs to the 'fat and bald-headed' figure of Simon Wheeler – speaks in the western vernacular. Boomerang is a fictional version of Angel's Camp in California, and the gold rush that spawned such towns only began in 1849. So Twain's use of the word 'ancient' to describe a recently-settled region looks to be a deliberate establishing of a quite different, and American, form of historical measurement. These factors help to explain something of the explosive impact of the sketch. For, as the New York correspondent of the San Francisco *Alta California* reported, Twain's story 'set all New York [where it was first published] in a roar. . . . It is voted the best thing of the day'.[3]

What did Twain's audiences find so funny about this sketch? It is difficult to imagine the conditions for the reception of a work written almost a century-and-a-half ago. But reading it now, it is still possible to see what made it (and still makes it) highly effective comedy. Simon Wheeler is the deadpan and apparently somewhat simple-minded remaining member of a once vibrant mining community, and has – we are told – 'an expression of winning gentleness and simplicity upon his tranquil countenance'. His voice carries the main narrative and Twain brilliantly creates here a representation of western vernacular speech, but one which is readily comprehensible to an American, and to any English-speaking, audience. Indeed it was Twain's ability to create forms of comedy that could easily cross national borders – he was more popular as a comic speaker in England than in America in the early years of his career – that helped to make him such a significant cultural figure. Twain retains all the distinctiveness of the western vernacular while losing nothing in clarity and accessibility. As Simon Wheeler starts to talk, in his disconcertingly digressive way, we are immediately caught up in his narrative web, waiting to see exactly where he is taking us.

The frame narrator of the story is 'Mark Twain'. It is he whose introduction and conclusion 'contain' Wheeler's tale and who has all the markings of genteel and educated, and therefore presumably eastern, origin. He starts by addressing his narrative to 'Mr. A. Ward' (Artemus Ward), who has apparently suggested this encounter: 'DEAR SIR: – Well, I called on good-natured, garrulous old Simon Wheeler, and I inquired after your friend Leonidas W. Smiley, as you requested me to do, and I hereunto append the result'. The said 'result' is that Wheeler backs his interrogator 'into a corner and blockaded me there with his chair', launching into a 'monotonous [and entirely straight-faced] narrative' which immediately departs from Twain's point and never gets back to it:

> There was a feller here once by the name of *Jim* Smiley, in the winter of
> '49 – or maybe it was the spring of '50 – I don't recollect exactly, some
> how, though what makes me think it was one or the other is because I
> remember the big flume wasn't finished when he first come to the camp;
> but anyway, he was the curiosest man about always betting on anything
> that turned up you ever see. . . .

Wheeler then tells a number of (cumulative) stories about (this) Smiley's betting exploits. As he does so, the markers of the vernacular speech get stronger (Twain introduces the reader to this speech gradually) and the comedy gets broader. This happens as we are given a series of condensed illustrations of Smiley and the various animals he bets on, and as Wheeler comically strains the boundaries of credibility both in the details of his tales and in the attribution of human characteristics to the animals concerned. One longish example will illustrate:

> Smiley . . . had a little small bull-pup, that to look at him you'd think he
> warn't worth a cent. . . . But as soon as money was up on him he was a
> different dog – his under-jaw'd begin to stick out like the for'castle of a
> steamboat, and his teeth would uncover, and shine savage like the
> furnaces. And a dog might tackle him, and bully-rag him, and bite
> him, . . . and Andrew Jackson – which was the name of the pup – . . . all
> of a sudden he would grab that other dog just by the joint of his hind leg
> and freeze to it . . . and hang on till they throwed up the sponge. . . .
> Smiley always came out winner on that pup till he harnessed a dog once
> that didn't have no hind legs, because they'd been sawed off in a circular
> saw, and when . . . he came to make a snatch for his pet holt, he saw in a
> minute how he'd been imposed on, . . . and then he looked sorter
> discouraged like, . . . and so he got shucked out bad. He gave Smiley a
> look as much to say his heart was broke, and it was *his* fault, for putting
> up a dog that hadn't no hind legs for him to take holt off, . . . and then he
> limped off a piece, and laid down and died.

This is followed by another example of unexpected reversal, when Smiley's trained jumping frog, Dan'l Webster, is beaten by a frog fetched out of the local swamp. This is done on behalf of a 'stranger in the camp' who bets on the newly-captured frog and whose comment on Dan'l Webster ('I don't see no points about that frog that's any better'n any other frog') would immediately pass into American popular usage and then to the national comic memory. The stranger fills Dan'l Webster with quail-shot while Smiley is away in the swamp with predictable results: when the contest starts 'Dan'l give a heave, and hysted up his shoulders – so – like a Frenchman, but it wasn't no use – . . . he was planted as solid as an anvil'. Wheeler then starts a story about Smiley's 'yaller one-eyed cow' but is interrupted by the narrator who makes his escape: '"O, curse Smiley and his afflicted cow!" I muttered, good-naturedly, and bidding the old gentleman good-day, I departed' (*TSSE1*, 171–7).

This sketch is short but brilliant. The individual sequences within the story are condensed comic masterpieces. But the whole sketch is about being hoaxed or taken-in and about the unexpected reversal of expectations. 'Mark Twain' is apparently hoaxed by Ward, set up for an encounter with Wheeler and his long-winded and meandering stories (Twain's skill should be noted here, the way he represents these qualities with such extreme economy). Wheeler may also be taking-in 'Mark Twain', may deliberately be frustrating this business-like and well-spoken eastern stranger by his digressions – for, in part, this is a story about community insiders and outsiders and who gets the better of whom. We can, however, never know whether Wheeler is in fact a skilled hoaxer or a naïve simpleton. But the reader too is being hoaxed here. For he or she cannot help but think that the stories Wheeler tells will have some final point to them. And it is only (sooner or later in the reading process) that s/he realises that the having of a final point is not the intention, either of Wheeler or of Twain the author. The series of miniature stories being told, rather, are to be enjoyed as comically self-sufficient in themselves and in their cumulative impact. This comedy of meandering indirection would always be a favourite weapon in Twain's comic armoury. The sketch is about trickery and misplaced trust, but it is also one in which the reader is left stranded and tricked, without a definitive way of interpreting what he or she reads. Is s/he meant to identify with 'Mark Twain' or with Wheeler and his point of view? Who is more trustworthy, or deserves our admiration or empathy: the stranger who cheats by filling Dan'l Webster with quail-shot, or Smiley, who takes on the stranger's challenge thinking that he is bound to win? Such comic indeterminacy is typical of the way Twain's best humour works.

To read through the complete range of Twain's travel writing and fiction is to encounter a wealth of memorable comic moments, some of a highly exuberant and even surreal, kind. 'Personal Habits of the Siamese Twins' (1869) explores one of Twain's favourite motifs, twin-ship. For he was always fascinated by this condition, and what it implied about the two related subjects of distinct individual identity and agency (the responsibility humans bear for their actions and the results of those actions). Twain based this short sketch on the real-life brothers from Siam, Chang and Eng, the original 'Siamese Twins'. They toured in the United States from 1828–39 as a circus exhibition – for part of the period under the management of P. T. Barnum (the famous American showman). They then settled in North Carolina and were married (to a pair of sisters – though not twins or physically interconnected) and, between them, went on to have twenty-one children. They died at age sixty-three, Eng evidently waking on the morning of 17 January 1874 to discover his brother dead beside him. One story has it that a doctor was sent for to separate the twins; another, that Eng would not countenance such a (suggested) separation. He died some three hours after his brother.

Twain's imagination was deeply affected by his knowledge of the twins. This early sketch is based on fact, but fact to which Twain added a series of comic twists and touches. Thus the twins' Siamese connection stimulates a poker-face and deliberately simple-minded description of the brothers' close companionship. This then develops into a mock philosophical and anthropological critique of man's alienation from his fellow man in a supposedly civilised and progressive society:

> Even as children [the Siamese Twins] were inseparable companions; and it was noticed that they always seemed to prefer each other's society to that of any other persons. They nearly always played together; and, so accustomed was their mother to this peculiarity, that, whenever both of them chanced to be lost, she usually only hunted for one of them – satisfied that when she found that one she would find his brother somewhere in the immediate neighborhood. And yet these creatures were ignorant and unlettered – barbarians themselves and the offspring of barbarians, who knew not the light of philosophy and science. What a withering rebuke is this to our boasted civilization, with its quarrelings, its wranglings, and its separations of brothers!

There are already clear signs here of the relativistic vision – the layering of one situation and point of view against another – that would form a crucial part of Twain's comic artillery and philosophical perspective.

Twain then cranks up the absurd elements in his sketch – for he would always rely on the humour of incongruity and of the mind-jarringly ludicrous, in his work. He begins with a statement which seems to offer the reader information into the Twins' way of life but which, in fact, is completely redundant given their Siamese connection: 'The Twins always go to bed at the same time'. Even as the reader takes this in, though, the introduction of the absurd provides a jolt to such a normative and rational understanding. For the sequence runs on: '. . . but Chang usually gets up about an hour before his brother. By an understanding between themselves, Chang does all the in-door work and Eng runs all the errands. This is because Eng likes to go out; Chang's habits are sedentary.' We then return to their linked physical state and its consequence, though here choice rather than necessity is implied: 'However, Chang always goes along.' The sketch ends in similar incongruity, but in a type of anti-climactic and illogical conclusion that Twain would often favour in his early years: 'Having forgotten to mention it sooner, I will remark, in conclusion, that the ages of the Siamese Twins are respectively fifty-one and fifty-three years' (*TSSE1*, 296–9).

There is more that could be said about this brief sketch, and indeed many of Twain's early short works might be similarly used to illustrate rich humour at work. But wherever we go in Twain we find both subtle and broad comedy realised in a large number of different ways. In *Innocents Abroad*, Twain constructs his persona – in one of his many guises – as a bumptious American tourist, under-awed by the cultural and historical heritage of Europe and the respect he is expected to show in such a presence. Travelling in Paris with 'the boys', a group of like-minded companions and under the direction of a guide they casually re-name 'Ferguson', the group are not taken to the Louvre, their intended destination, but to one silk store after another, where they might disburse their tourist dollars. 'The doctor', one of Twain's companions, responds with a (typical) poker-faced irony to the situation and one which deliberately plays on the image of the American abroad as both ignorant and naive:

> Within fifteen minutes the carriage halted again, and before another silk store. The doctor said:
> 'Ah, the palace of the Louvre; beautiful, beautiful edifice! Does the Emperor Napoleon live here now, Ferguson?'   (121)

Twain then rails at the Parisian guides who 'deceive and defraud every American who goes to Paris for the first time', and raises the spectre of future revenge: 'I shall visit Paris again some day, and then let the guides beware! I shall go in my war-paint – I shall carry my tomahawk along' (123–4).

Twain was generally less than sympathetic to the American Indian. But here the persona of avenging 'savage' suits his purposes ideally, opposed as it is to a European high culture and sophistication (usually presented as a fraud or as a concealment for less-than-admirable motives and actions). The illustration 'Return in War-Paint' accompanies the passage, and was used to promote the book. It shows Twain dressed in Indian leggings and tunic, but with a jacket over the latter and a shirt and tie beneath. He has a bow and arrow on his back, and feathers in his (more conventionally western) hat. He carries a tomahawk in one hand and a satchel, with 'MT' and 'US' stamped on it, in the other. This representation of a hybrid part-Indian American self suits his nationalistic purposes here: Twain would not often identify himself with such a 'barbaric' extreme.

The doctor's intentionally absurd question about Napoleon is echoed in a whole series of disruptive comic tactics that Twain and the boys call on throughout their trip, all introduced to debunk any assumption of European cultural superiority. The best known of these is the response they use whenever their guides refer to a famous historical or artistic personage. Another 'Ferguson' (this time in Genoa) shows the boys a 'beautiful, O, magnificent bust Christopher Columbo . . . ze great Christopher Columbo!' The boys then go into their now normal routine, to the discomfiture of their guide's expectations and assumptions:

> The doctor put up his eye-glass – procured for such occasions. . . .
>   'Christopher Columbo – the great Christopher Columbo. Well, what did *he* do?'
>   'Discover America! – discover America, Oh, ze devil!'
>   'Discover America. No – that statement will hardly wash. We are just from America ourselves. We heard nothing about it. Christopher Columbo – pleasant name – is – is he dead?'   (292).

If Columbus was the explorer who first established an American debt to, and cultural dependency on, Europe, Twain's modern and independent Americans symbolically rid themselves of that influence as they pretend not even to know his name.

The formula used here has slight variations as it is repeated in the book but it is always used to the same end. Thus, subject to the viewing of innumerable painting and frescoes by Michelangelo in Rome, the doctor asks the inevitable question when they are then taken to the Roman Forum:

> 'Michael Angelo?'
> A stare from the guide. 'No – thousan' year before he is born'.
> Then an Egyptian obelisk. Again: 'Michael Angelo?'
>   'Oh, *mon dieu*, genteelmen! . . . .'   (289)

The routine continues as the group is taken to see 'a royal Egyptian mummy' in the Vatican museums:

> 'See, genteelmen! – Mummy! Mummy!'
> '. . . How calm he is – how self-possessed. Is, ah – is he dead?'
> 'Oh, *sacre bleu*, been dead three thousan' year!'
> The doctor turned on him savagely:
>
> > 'Here, now, what do you mean by such conduct as this! Playing us for Chinamen because we are strangers and trying to learn! Trying to impose your vile second-hand carcasses on *us!* – thunder and lightning,

I've a notion to – to – if you've got a nice *fresh* corpse, fetch him out! –
or, by George, we'll brain you!'   (294)

This is of course a deliberately exaggerated ethnocentric humour, but it is no
less funny for that. The mixture of macabre relish and threatened violence at the
end of the sequence suggests the difficulties of controlling and containing such
a bumptious and irreverent American presence in this ritualised Old World
context.

Perhaps the examples of Twain's comic imagination with which today's readers are most familiar come from *The Adventures of Tom Sawyer*. Tom Sawyer's
boyhood resistance to the world of adult (and predominantly female) domesticity and propriety form a good part of the book's appeal – especially, perhaps,
to male readers. Dressed for Sunday School, a 'place that [he] hated with his
whole heart', and galled by the 'restraint' that such 'whole clothes and cleanliness' bring with them (45), Tom, nonetheless is keen to compete there for
a Bible. This is awarded in exchange for the coloured tickets given for the
memorising of its verses. He gathers the requisite number (equivalent to two
thousand verses), and longs for 'the glory, and the eclat' (46) that is to come
with the achievement. Being Tom Sawyer, however, he will always – when given
the chance – short-circuit and undermine set institutional procedures and the
conventional value systems on which they are based: in this case, religious
education and book-learning.

Rather than learning his verses, Tom has built up the necessary number of
tokens through trade. So, for instance, he gets a yellow ticket by exchanging
a 'piece of lickrish and a fish-hook' for it (45) – objects of some value in his
alternative boy-world. The worldly figure of the 'great Judge Thatcher', who is
to present the Bible to Tom, mouths the conventional pieties and congratulates
him on the 'trouble you took to learn [the verses]; for knowledge is worth
more than anything there is in the world' (51). He then, however, asks Tom
publicly to repeat the names of the first two disciples Christ appointed. Tom
looks sheepish but, prompted by the Judge's wife, blurts out his answer:

'Now, I know you'll tell *me*' said the lady. 'The names of the first two
disciples were – '
'DAVID AND GOLIAH!'

'Let us', the narrator then concludes the chapter, 'draw the curtain of charity
over the rest of the scene' (52).

The humour in the scene is produced by a number of complementary effects.
It depends on the extreme, dramatic and very public nature of Tom's error; and

on the gaps between the two worlds (boyhood and adult) and their respective value schemes (play and pleasure, prayer and hard work). But it is also heightened by Twain's satiric prompts that both worlds have their similarities, in particular, a certain delight in self-importance and a general love of 'showing-off'. Other set-pieces in the book – the white-washing of Aunt Polly's fence, the loosing of the 'pinch-bug' in church, Tom's attendance at his own funeral – use related techniques to produce similarly effective comic results.

American naiveté and ignorance play a large part in producing the comic effects in *Innocents Abroad*. Those same characteristics reappear in *Huckleberry Finn*. In Huck's case, however, the ignorance is real rather than an assumed mask. One example of the humour thus produced, from the early chapters of the novel – when Huck is living under Miss Watson's oppressive regime – will serve to illustrate. Miss Watson gives Huck a 'good going-over', on account of his 'greased up and clayey' clothes, the product of an illicit night out spent with Tom Sawyer. She then (in Huck's words):

> took me in the closet and prayed, but nothing come of it. She told me to pray every day, and whatever I asked for I would get it. But it warn't so. I tried it. Once I got a fish-line, but no hooks. It warn't any good to me without hooks. I tried for the hooks three or four times, but somehow I couldn't make it work. By-and-by, one day, I asked Miss Watson to try for me, but she said I was a fool. She never told me why, and I couldn't make it out no way.
>
> I set down, one time, back in the woods, and had a long think about it. I says to myself, if a body can get anything they pray for, why don't Deacon Winn get back the money he lost on pork? Why can't the widow get back her silver snuff-box that was stole? Why can't Miss Watson fat up? No, says I to myself, there ain't nothing in it. I went and told the widow about it, and she said the thing a body could get by praying for it was 'spiritual gifts'. This was too many for me, but she told me what she meant – I must help other people, . . . and look out for them all the time, and never think about myself. This was including Miss Watson, as I took it. I went out in the woods and turned it over in my mind a long time, but I couldn't see no advantage about it – except for the other people – so at last I reckoned I wouldn't worry about it any more, but just let it go.   (28–30)

The humour here works simply, but resonates in more complex ways, something typical of Twain's book. The young boy, Huck, is more used to living in a sugar hogs-head, dressed in old rags, than with the 'dismal regular and decent' (17) Widow Douglas and her sister Miss Watson. We here follow his thought processes and actions as he tries to make sense of the rituals and expectations of the two women's respectable lives. The idea of praying in the closet (defined in the 1858 *Webster's Dictionary* as 'any room for privacy – 'When thou prayest enter into thy *closet*'. – Matt. vi.) suggests a separation between secular and spiritual life. This will be of crucial importance to a novel in which Miss Watson's everyday status as a slave-holder (like that of her fellow Southerners) fails to square with basic Christian principles: to 'look out for [other people] all the time'. It also, though, introduces a notion of separate spheres for different types of activity, something that only confuses Huck, who does not divide up life in such a way.

Huck, throughout the novel, reports straightforwardly on what he sees, acts pragmatically and takes things literally. He consequently sees no humour in praying for fishing tackle once he has been told that 'whatever I asked for I would get it'. His patience and persistence in praying for the fish-hooks is a measure of his naiveté (by the reader's standard) and his literalism. Miss Watson's dismissive response to these prayers ('she said I was a fool') covers up her potential difficulty in explaining the difference between material and 'spiritual gifts', self-interest and the welfare of others and why prayer should only be effective in one of these realms. The humour of the situation exists in Huck's inability to see what any religious person would take for granted. But it is precisely his knack of looking at things afresh and the defamiliarisations that occur (allowing the reader also to see things from a completely new and alternative perspective), that give his character and his voice so much power in the novel – a power that contrasts with his complete social powerlessness. And the hypocrisies of Christian behaviour, at least as illustrated by Miss Watson and her like, will become the eventual target of Twain's critique, through the medium of Huck's words and actions. Better to pray for fish-hooks and treat African Americans as full human beings (as Huck comes to do) than to pray for spiritual betterment and treat them as mere property.

Huck's puzzled contemplation, sitting back in the woods, of the things others take for granted but that he fails to understand, also has its comic elements. From the viewpoint of a social 'insider' who recognises how the world works, including the world of conventional religious practice, it is Huck's naiveté and the type of questions he asks himself, that create the humour. As a pragmatist, Huck is interested in concrete results: the recovery of the silver snuff-box. (We recall here that the widow tells Huck that his smoking is 'a mean practice and wasn't clean' – her snuff-taking, though, 'of course . . . was all right, because she done it herself', 18–19). Similarly, he wonders why Miss Watson cannot 'fat up'. The brevity and colloquial vigour of the last phrase and its suggestion, perhaps, of a possible easy physicality and comfort checked, in Miss Watson's case, by an abstemious self-discipline, contains its own comic charge.

Huck's final analysis of what he has been told – that he can't see 'no advantage to it' so will 'just let it go' – also acts to release comedy for the reader, though not for Huck (who remains serious throughout). This stems from his complete alienation from standard ways of viewing religious practice, a final incomprehension of its ways and the gesture of total non-judgmental disaffiliation that follows: one of 'let them go their way, I'll go mine'. The sequence prepares the reader for the whole book. For in it, conventional Christianity and the relation between its theory and practice in a slave-holding South will be subject to critique. Pragmatic action based on the immediate situation will be contrasted with action based on inherited and conventional social or religious assumptions. And the possibility of stepping outside the normal social framework, both mentally and physically (in the hogs-head, on the island and raft, 'light[ing] out for the Territory') will always be kept open.

Twain's humour changes tack in *A Connecticut Yankee*, though again it is often driven by an unbridgeable divide between different ways of thinking and acting. For much of its comedy is released in the tension between Hank Morgan's modern American identity and the pre-modern ways of the Arthurian England to which he finds himself transported. When Hank, head superintendent in Sam Colt's Hartford arms factory, is 'laid . . . out with a crusher [from a crowbar] alongside the head' by one of the 'rough men' working under him (20–1), he wakes to find himself in sixth-century England. Judging himself a 'master intelligence among intellectual moles' (102), he quickly gains power (as 'Sir Boss') and introduces nineteenth-century technology and business practice to the kingdom. The juxtapositions between the two worlds (sixth- and nineteenth-century), and the anachronistic and sometimes surreal effects that result, provide a ready source of humour in the novel.

Hank's imperialist agenda literally brings the twinned benefits of 'soap and civilization' (191) to a backward world. He sends out the bravest knights in the kingdom as 'missionaries' (190) for the modernised social and industrial order he wishes to introduce, advertising his 'improvements' (532) on the sandwich-boards he has them carry. Approaching Morgan Le Fay's castle, Hank meets one of his emissaries whose boards read, 'Persimmon's Soap – All the Prime-Donne Use It' (190): a message aimed at the Arthurian lack of even 'rudimentary cleanliness' (191). There is already a linguistic joke in having a word that usually connotes temperamental female behaviour used both slyly and anachronistically in this setting. But the main comedy lies in the absurdist meld of old and new. Knight-errantry (with its chivalric and dignified associations) meets the hard-selling techniques of a commerce-driven world here, in a figure now made ridiculous through the combination of plumed helmet and steel dress with the stiff, square advertising-hoarding.

The joke is then ratcheted up a level, as Hank describes his missionary's routine: to 'explain to the lords and ladies [he encounters] what soap was; and if the lords and ladies were afraid of it, get them to try it on a dog' (191). In this particular case, his envoy is 'much depressed', having 'not worked off a cake [of soap]; yet he had tried all the tricks of his trade, even to the washing of a hermit; but the hermit died'. Hank's business mind looks to convert this apparent failure into a campaign victory since, to his thinking, 'for such as have brains there are no defeats, but only victories'. He accordingly adds the words, 'Patronized by the Elect', to the knight's board. Hank's self-congratulation is well-justified: 'for just a modest little one-liner ad., it's a corker' (193). Quite apart from his comic foresight in anticipating the language, tactics and morality (or rather, the lack of it) of the advertising business, Twain uses his final gag brilliantly, with its perfect crossing of the commercial and religious divide.

Similar tactics of representing two different worlds in comic collision are used where Hank hooks up a renowned hermit in the Valley of Holiness to a sewing-machine. Noting the hermit's ceaseless 'bowing [of] his body' ('1244 revolutions in 24 minutes and 46 seconds' by the stop-watch), and reluctant to 'have all this power going to waste', Hank arranges to rig up 'a system of elastic cords' to channel the man's movements to the running of his machine. This enables him to produce and sell shirts:

> I . . . got five years' good service out of him; in which time he turned out upwards of eighteen thousand first-rate tow-linen shirts, which was ten a day. I worked him Sundays and all; he was going, Sundays, the same as week-days, and it was no use to waste the power. These shirts . . . sold like smoke to pilgrims at a dollar and a half apiece . . . [and] were regarded as a perfect protection against sin. . . .
>
> But . . . I [later] noticed that the motive power had taken to standing on one leg, . . . so I stocked the business and unloaded. . . . [T]he works stopped within a year, and the good saint got him to his rest. But he had earned it. I can say that for him.   (280–2)

Again here, the discourse and assumptions of commerce clash with those of religion. Having a totally secular mind-set, Hank has no hesitation in making use of religious devotion and superstitious belief to his own material ends.

Humour emerges in the visual images called up by his descriptions but also, in a more blackly-comic fashion, in the way that Hank's rationalisations (and the time-and-motion study that supports them) convert the human materials he uses into a type of mechanical object, much like the sewing-machine to which that human being is physically linked.

This suggests the way that in this novel, too, Twain's comedy is intimately connected to more serious themes. Hank's rationalising late-nineteenth-century business mind selfishly uses the human beings at his disposal. He presents himself as the political agent of democratic values and liberty, but his actions chain the subjects he would represent to a form of industrial slavery (and one, in this case, without any wage bills attached). Twain's doubts about modernisation and its values and his growing insistence that human nature consists of a mixture of self-interest (Hank's in this case) and blind ignorance (the hermit's) are both illustrated here. Accordingly, his comedy takes an altogether darker tone than it generally previously had.

But Twain, even toward the end of his career, retained his capacity for sheer comic exuberance. In 'A Double-Barreled Detective Story' (1902), he takes clear delight in burlesquing Conan Doyle's Sherlock Holmes. He makes considerable broad comic play, too, out of the bloodhound characteristic, an extraordinary sense of smell, apparently inherited by his protagonist, Archy Stillman, from (in what for the author was a very risqué move) his sexually abused mother. By and large, though, Twain's vision did become more pessimistic as he aged, and his comedy darkened accordingly.

As this happened, his humorous writing turned in two main directions. The first was toward the kind of biting irony to be found in 'The Man That Corrupted Hadleyburg' (1899), with a view of human behaviour as consisting predominantly of self-interested hypocrisy and greed. We might recall here Twain's own denial of any caste, creed or colour prejudice in 'Concerning the Jews' (1899) where he writes: 'All that I care to know is that a man is a human being – that is enough for me; he can't be any worse' (*TSSE2*, 355).

The other and alternative direction his humour takes is toward what a modern generation (but not Twain's own) would call black humour – a mode of humour that makes a joke of the assumption that life has any definite purpose, or that the universe makes any real sense. The comic relativism to be found in so much late Twain rests on such a conceptual base. (Similar forms of humour, it should be said, are also found earlier. Any reading that looks to completely divide his writing career into discrete and separate stages does not entirely work.) As an example of Twain's work that (almost) fits this black humour pattern – and the 'almost' is important – we might look at 'Was the World Made for Man?' published posthumously in *Letters from the Earth* (1962). Twain was clearly very familiar with Darwinian thought and in this short piece he queries – as did so many in his time – the compatibility of evolutionary theory and Christian providentialism (the idea that God has a special plan or providence in mind for the human race). But he goes one step beyond this, too, to ask whether the very idea of an upward-moving evolutionary progression (at least in anything but the history of physical organisms) makes much sense.

Addressing his title question, Twain maps the evolutionary chain that has led to man's appearance: 'It takes a long time to prepare a world for man, such a thing is not done in a day'. Starting with the early invertebrates, he soon (in terms of the development of his own argument, at any rate) reaches the oyster and it is at that point that his comic relativism – with a passing barb aimed at scientific logic – begins to become apparent:

> An oyster has hardly any more reasoning power than a scientist has, and so it is reasonably certain that this one jumped to the conclusion that the nineteen million years [of previous early life-forms] was a preparation for *him*; but that would be just like an oyster, which is the most conceited animal there is, except man.

Then, working his way through fish, dinosaurs, birds, kangaroos, giant sloths and Irish elks, Twain recreates a comic, but loosely accurate, version of the evolutionary chain, until he reaches the monkey. This is where his sketch ends:

> And at last came the monkey, and anybody could see that man wasn't far off, now. And in truth that was so. The monkey went on developing for close upon five million years, and then turned into a man – to all appearances.
>
> Such is the history of it. Man has been here 32,000 years. That it took a hundred million years to prepare the world for him is proof that that is what it was done for. I suppose it is. I dunno. If the Eiffel Tower were now representing the world's age, the skin of paint on the pinnacle-knob at its summit would represent man's share of that age; and anybody would perceive that that skin was what the tower was built for. I reckon they would, I dunno.   (*LE*, 166–70)

The very idea of evolution, either in terms of a providential scheme with man at the universe's centre or in terms of progressive improvement in intellectual or moral power (see that 'to all appearances' above) is thrown into relativistic comic doubt. And yet . . . ? Twain is uncertain about the position he takes, as the repeated 'I dunno' suggests. There is something here that strains against the lack of human or anthropological/historical meaning he would seem comically to propose. And this is typical of an author who could never be completely comfortable in either the pessimism or the comic (and sometimes cosmic) relativism that mark his final years.

Travel and travel writing: *Innocents Abroad, A Tramp Abroad, Roughing It, Life on the Mississippi*

Despite his reputation as one of the most 'American' of writers, Twain is a key figure in any account of the cultural connections and exchanges across national and international borders in his period. If his humour first came out of the American frontier, it proved immediately popular with a British audience. When Twain first visited England in August 1872, he was widely fêted, and found himself already well-known: 'a lion', 'by long odds the most widely known & popular American author among the English' (*L5*, 184, 197). Very much at home there, he wrote home to wife Olivia: 'Too much company – too much dining – too much sociability. (But I would rather live in England than America – which is treason.)' (*L5*, 155). He made his visit in the first place in part to gather material for a book provisionally titled *Upon the Oddities and Eccentricities of the English*. But the genuine warmth of his reception in the country helped persuade him to abandon this project. And by the end of 1873 he had visited England three times, thoroughly enjoying his reputation there as author, lecturer and wit.

Indeed, it would seem that the British public recognised Twain's exceptional comic talents and gave him celebrity status, more quickly than his native audience. Albert Bigelow Paine, his biographer, spoke of him being treated as 'little less than royalty' (*L5*, 372) on his second English visit in May–October 1873. Twain quickly followed this up with a third trip (November 1873–January 1874) to deliver a further series of lectures. After photographs were taken of him, apparently to go on sale to the general public, he wrote to Olivia that: 'it seems as if 3 out of every 5 I meet on the street recognize me. This in London! It seems incredible' (*L5*, 532).

What is noteworthy here is just how appreciative a nineteenth-century British audience was of a form of humour that one might assume was culturally alien to it. Contemporary British reports of Twain's new lecture on 'Roughing It on the Silver Frontier' spoke of the audience's initial ignorance of the 'locality to which he intended to introduce them' ('Mexico was generally suggested'). But they nonetheless described both the success of Twain's comic material and his distinctive way of delivering it. As Moncure Daniel Conway wrote (around the turn of 1873–4): 'The talk of literary London just now is Mark Twain's account, in his new lecture of the "bucking" horse which he purchased in Nevada. It is impossible to put it on paper, as half of the effect produced by the story depends upon his manner of telling it' (see *L5*, 507).

We tend to think of comedy and of literary performances generally (in Twain's case, both lectures and fiction) as limited and culture-specific forms. But we also recognise that, in the hands of their best practitioners, their appeal transcends national boundaries – so, for instance, Charles Dickens's popularity in the America of his time. Twain's comedy proved, from the first, capable of such cross-national cultural work. And as he made the shift from comic sketch and lecture to longer – and more complex – fictional writing, he retained his international appeal. As time has passed, that appeal has grown to make Twain one of the best-known world literary figures. A recent translation of 'Eve's Diary' and 'Extracts from Adam's Diary' into Japanese, for example, sold some 230,000 copies.[4]

More work remains to be done on how to account for a popularity that seems to take so little account of national borderlines. It may be that once authors and texts are established as canonical in the English-speaking world, their larger circulation becomes more likely. Or it may be that certain forms of humour transcend certain culture-specific boundaries. Or perhaps, in the case of novels like *Tom Sawyer* and *Huckleberry Finn*, the pre-modernist settings and the focus on a boyhood world that (in some ways) escapes adult constriction carry their own broad transcultural appeal. The mythic archetypes the texts tap into – death and fearful night-time villainy, the cave and the hidden treasure, in *Tom Sawyer*; river, raft and shore, slavery and freedom, civilisation and the escape from its constrictions, in its sequel – then reinforce such an appeal. (I interrogate the apparent simplicity of such oppositional patterns later in the book.) The deeper levels of moral and social meaning which resonate in *Huckleberry Finn* may also speak to parallel or related concerns in quite different cultural contexts.

To consider Twain's international reputation and audience in his own time is also to note just how much time he spent outside America. It is to recognise, too, how much of what he wrote was either set in Europe (and beyond) or addressed issues of transnational concern. This was clearly true of the three non-American travel books. But *The Prince and the Pauper, Connecticut Yankee, Joan of Arc,* and *No. 44, The Mysterious Stranger* are all, additionally, located outside his country.

Twain's own travels abroad started as a newspaper correspondent in the Sandwich Islands in 1866. He acted in the same role on the 1867 *Quaker City* cruise to Europe and the Holy Land, the trip then described in *The Innocents Abroad*. The early English visits are noted above. In 1878, he took his family with him as he visited continental Europe and gathered material for *A Tramp Abroad*. And from 1891 to late 1900, Twain and his family were virtual expatriates, staying in a large number of European cities and villages. Perhaps the most significant of these stays, from an artistic point of view, was spent in and near Vienna from September 1897 to May 1899, a highly productive period for him generally. That series of European residencies was broken by his round-the-world lecture tour in 1895–6. After some years back in America, he then returned to Italy, to Florence, in 1903, looking for relief for Olivia's health problems in the congenial climate. Her death there marked the end of Twain's European visits, excepting a last short and triumphal English trip in the summer of 1907 to receive an honorary degree from Oxford University.

Twain's reasons for spending so much time in Europe were, in part, for literary reasons (collecting new material for his books), but he had a series of other motives too. The high costs of living and entertaining in the Hartford house made European travel, paradoxically, into an economy. It also served, on at least one occasion, as an escape from an embarrassment at home. For Twain's comic irreverence, combined with mannerisms and behaviour that were the product of a very different early environment than the majority of his genteel Hartford and Boston friends and acquaintances, meant that he was always likely to commit social misdemeanours of various types.

One famous breach of etiquette took place with Twain's 'Whittier Birthday Speech' of 17 December 1877. Speaking at the seventieth-birthday celebrations of respected New England poet, John Greenleaf Whittier, Twain told a comic tale in which Whittier along with Ralph Waldo Emerson and Henry Wadsworth Longfellow (fellow New England cultural 'worthies' and also at the banquet) were represented in burlesque form, as three uncouth and brawling drunks assumed their identities in a California mining-camp setting. The joke seems to have fallen on stony ground (though Howell's remembrance of it as a 'disaster' seems an overstatement). The event, though, takes on real symbolic importance if it is seen in terms of a cocky, western and far-from-genteel voice mocking the elderly representatives of an eastern and high-toned literary establishment, at the very point that the balance of literary power in the nation was changing. But it seems to have embarrassed Twain enough to have been at least one of the reasons for his temporary move to Europe in 1878.

Motives for his various trips abroad, then, differed (see Chapter 1). Twain seems himself to have found Europe something of an escape and relief from an America with which he was increasingly disillusioned. But the trips there formed one part of more extended foreign travels. He visited Hawaii as a journalist in 1866 and saw significant parts of North Africa and the Middle East on the *Quaker City* cruise. The 1895–6 round-the-world lecture tour – which took in Australia, New Zealand, India, and South Africa (among other countries) – gave Twain a first-hand experience of a larger world quite extraordinary for a popular American writer in his period. He was in Bermuda (one of his favourite places) for his health in 1910, when his heart condition became so severe that he had, in effect, to be fetched home to die.

The Innocents Abroad

Twain's first full-length book, *The Innocents Abroad or The New Pilgrim's Progress* (1869) was a travel narrative. It was this work that fully launched him on his career as a professional writer and this was the genre to which he would return at intervals throughout his life. Critics in the past have tended to downplay the travel books in favour of an emphasis on the major novels. But there has been renewed interest in such works and their general cultural context in recent years.[5] This interest is in large part a product of the transnational turn in American Studies: the understanding that American history and culture cannot be examined in a vacuum but are part of, and inseparable from, larger international movements and cross-cultural currents and influences. I explore this critical approach more fully in Chapter 7.

Such cross-cultural interests and effects in *Innocents Abroad* can be immediately briefly illustrated. Twain describes how his 'young and green' companion buttonholes some 'educated British Officers' in Gibraltar 'and badgers them with braggadocio about America and the wonders she can perform' (71). A few pages later, Twain enters the 'packed and jammed city' of Tangier and speaks of its 'uncompromisingly foreign' nature. 'More than a thousand years old', it is inhabited by 'stalwart Bedouins of the desert . . . , and stately Moors, proud of a history that goes back to the night of time; and Jews, whose fathers fled hither centuries upon centuries ago; and . . . original, genuine negroes, as black as Moses' (76–8). There are a number of elements in this last description that ask his American readers to check their standard assumptions, even to re-think their own sense of national identity. Twain's reference to 'Moses the black' (or Moses the Ethiopian) is an immediate reminder of the mixed racial history of Christianity – that it cannot be automatically coded 'white'. While his phrase 'genuine negroes' points (whether consciously or not) toward the hybrid nature of *African American* 'negroes' – culturally formed by their American world as well as by any prior heritage, whose skin colour too was often the product of racial mixing. Indeed, the phrase might provide an oblique reference to the larger, and even more hybrid, sense of 'American' national identity as a whole (for, in what from the first was an immigrant nation, who or what is a 'genuine' American?). The juxtaposition of these two sequences, however, clearly implies the shortcomings of New World confidence and bumptiousness in their encounters with a much older and historically complex world. Moreover, there is a suggestion of the cultural need to bridge, in some way, that 'uncompromising' gap described. Twain's account never loses sight of the different set of assumptions and values to be found both in Europe and the Middle East and his sense of his own 'American' identity cannot be divorced from such cross-cultural comparison and exchange.

Elsewhere, however, 'Mark Twain', the protagonist of *Innocents*, shares much of his greenhorn compatriot's braggadocio. This indicates something of the many contradictions in this text. To understand, for example, why the book was so enormously popular on its first appearance is to focus on the very assertive and new sense of American national identity which it, in part, promotes. Twain's opening description of his trip is as a 'great Pleasure Excursion', 'a picnic on a gigantic scale', where – among a host of other activities – the participants 'were to hob-nob with nobility and hold friendly converse with kings and princes' (19–20). This immediately denies the high seriousness and quest for cultural knowledge traditionally associated with past American visitors to Europe. Instead it assumes that an easy-going pleasure can be found there and brings an assured sense of democratic equality and familiarity to the experience.

The Civil War may have only recently ended (four years before publication) but there is scarcely a reference to it in Twain's book. Instead, there is an optimistic sense of an America looking forward, not backward. This complements the new-found national spending power and accompanying explosion of tourist activity that marked the immediate post-bellum period. Twain may satirise the patriotic routines of the shipboard Fourth of July celebration. But his references to the 'national flag', the Declaration of Independence, 'Hail Columbia', and 'The Star-Spangled Banner' (92) finally share the strongly patriotic note of that communal cheer raised when the Stars and Stripes, the 'country's flag', is seen flying from a passing ship (64). As we saw in the last chapter, Twain identifies himself with an Indian warrior (with war-paint and tomahawk) as he fulminates against fraudulent tourist guides. In doing so, he opposes wily European practices to native American assertiveness, simplicity and strength.

Twain comes to Europe to see the place afresh and with 'his own eyes instead of the eyes of those who travelled in those countries before . . .' (Preface). The history of travel and of travel writing has generally distinguished between 'travellers' and 'tourists'. Travellers are conventionally seen as '"nonexploitative" visitors, motivated not by the lazy desire for instant entertainment, but by [a deep] . . . curiosity about other countries and people.' '"Mere" tourists', on the other hand, are the 'vulgar herd' that follow in their footsteps.[6] If this is so, then Twain is happy to be a tourist, 'only want[ing] to glance and go – to move, keep moving!' (97).

In this role, Twain's tastes tend to veer away from high culture. He certainly has little time for the accepted treasures of the European art world. Da Vinci's 'The Last Supper', 'the most celebrated painting in the world' which Twain sees in Milan, has – for him – none of the aura, that special originality and once-in-a-lifetime radiance, conventionally associated with great art. He sees only a 'mournful wreck', its 'colors . . . dimmed with age', and much prefers the copies others artists make of it to the original itself (190–1). And if he wonders whether his lack of appreciation is something to do with the very abundance of such paintings on view, he still casually refers to 'the rubbish left by the old masters' (304). Christopher Newman, the protagonist of Henry James's *The American* (1877) visits the Louvre in 1868, the year after Twain's *Innocents Abroad* trip. He too – looking at the copies of the paintings made by 'innumerable young women . . . who devote themselves . . . to the propagation of masterpieces' – admits that 'if the truth must be told' he often admires 'the copy much more than the original.' Unlike Twain's protagonist, though, Newman finds himself inspired 'for the first time in his life, with a vague self-mistrust' by this reaction.[7]

This 'Mark Twain' (I once more stress the gap between the author and the first-person protagonist who also bears his name), however, reacts with an assertive nationalism. There is little of Newman's self-mistrust here. For he is quick to dismiss the majority of European practices and pretensions, and generally views all foreigners through xenophobic eyes. The people of Naples are 'filthy in their habits' (316) and Italians generally are characterised by their 'garlic-exterminating mouth[s]' (184). In Magdala, in Syria, once the Holy Land is reached, Twain describes how the 'stupid population . . . came trooping out' when his party of pilgrims arrive, 'all abject beggars by nature, instinct and education . . . vermin-tortured vagabonds' (504).

Civilisation is traditionally associated with soap, but this commodity cannot be had in the Milan public bath-house Twain and the boys visit. Thus Dan, one of Twain's buddies, looking to have the missing soap provided, calls out to the female attendant: 'Oh, bring some soap. . . . S-o-a-p, soap; s-o-p-e, soap; s-o-u-p, soap. Hurry up! I don't know how you Irish spell it, but I want it'. But, however loud and insistent the demands, the soap fails to arrive – 'there was good reason for it. There was not such an article about the establishment . . . [and] never had been' (188). There is no dialogue or proper translation here, only command. Moreover, most of the various exchanges in which Twain and his fellow-travellers engage are financially driven: the American dollar the sign of their privileged and exploitative authority. Twain's combative sense of American cultural identity is clearly evident, too, in his religious and political opinions. He makes dismissive remarks on many such matters, including Catholic superstition, the gap between the Church's wealth and the poverty of its congregation and the oppressive and autocratic forms of European political authority.

But there is much more to *Innocents Abroad* than its irreverence, its proclamations of American self-confidence and superiority and its rejection of large parts of Europe's rich cultural heritage. For at many points in the text (including the Milan bath-house episode above), it is clear that the author is strongly aware of the bigoted and blinkered nature of his naïve protagonist ('Mark Twain') and holds him at an obvious ironic remove. The celebration of a self-confident American identity with no need for lessons from the Old World past is one important part of the narrative, but it runs alongside a different (and more critical) perspective. The book is far from coherent in the value-schemes it represents, but that is no necessary surprise. For Twain was rarely straightforward in his vision and – in this particular case – similar fissures and tensions tend to mark any representation of American national character and ideology.

For, however much the American would present himself as a new man (or 'Newman' as James's representative protagonist is called), the past and Europe cannot just be ignored, or abandoned as irrelevant and unimportant. As Twain relaxes in Bellagio, in Italy, he speaks of going to bed:

> with drowsy brains harassed with a mad panorama that mixes up pictures of France, of Italy, of the ship, of the ocean, of home, in grotesque and bewildering disorder. Then a melting away of familiar faces, of cities and of tossing waves, into a great calm of forgetfulness and peace.
>   After which, the nightmare.   (201)

This is an odd and unusual passage, particularly in its final move from 'calm' to 'nightmare'. What comes over strongly here, though, is that travel in Europe affects any settled idea of the America 'home' – that this native country is necessarily seen afresh through, and even defamiliarised by, the foreign experience.

This can work in a simple and comparative way, whereby America and what it signifies and stands for is measured in terms of its difference from Europe and what is seen there. Throughout *Innocents Abroad*, Twain's readings of the two places are interdependent, judging and understanding the one against the other. Thus, on the one hand American 'stage-coaching' is associated with a sense of pleasurable freedom, escape from urban crowding, and of democratic privilege and value: 'it was worth a lifetime of city toiling and moiling . . . to scan the blue distances of a world that knew no lords but us'. Its full worth emerges only, though, as it is compared to the more tedious travel of 'railroading' in an 'elegant France', with no 'antelopes and buffaloes, and painted Indians on the war path' to stimulate the imagination. On the other, the helpful courtesies of the French railway officials are contrasted to the 'discommoding' self-regard of the 'railroad conductor of America'. And the measured and civilised breaks for dinner in the French system are compared to the 'five-minute boltings of flabby rolls, muddy coffee, [and] questionable eggs' in America (106–9). The achievements and failures of both cultures come into sharper focus as they are measured in their comparative difference.

Similarly, when Twain reaches Rome he judges there to be nothing 'for me to see that others have not seen before me'. The weight of other past responses to the city presses down on him in an overwhelming and stifling manner. But what he does see stimulates an extended recognition of the benefits of the American political and social system: 'a country . . . [with] no overshadowing Mother Church . . . common men and common women who could read . . . real glass windows in the houses of even the commonest people' (267–8). Even as he praises his native country, though, he reveals its faults:

> [In America] if a man be rich, he is very greatly honored, and can become a legislator, a governor, a general, a senator, no matter how ignorant an ass he is – just as in . . . Italy the nobles hold all the great places, even though sometimes they are born noble idiots.   (268)

American identity then is never absolute and free-floating and must always be read against European identity – and vice-versa. Travel brings cross-cultural self-evaluation (and re-evaluation) as a necessary part of its experience.

Moreover, knowledge and respect for European culture and for the Holy Land and its religious heritage are so strongly built into American cultural identity that – despite his iconoclasm – Twain often finds himself repeating conventional pieties, and echoing standard forms of response. He lapses into (and plagiarises) standard guide-book-speak, even – as he describes Versailles, with its 'vast fountains . . . discharg[ing] rivers of sparkling water into the air . . . in forms of matchless beauty', with its 'wide grass-carpeted avenues . . . and . . . glimpses of sylvan lakes' (153) – ending with the type of conventional archaism found in such a rhetoric. 'The old Venice of song and story' is recaptured on the Grand Canal, as 'under the mellow moonlight the Venice of poetry and romance stood revealed' (218). Pompeii prompts thoughts of the ineradicable nature of the human past. The handprints hollowed in stone close beside a drinking spout cause Twain to address the reader in reverent and sentimental wonder: 'Think of the countless thousands of hands that had pressed that spot in the ages that are gone, to so reduce a stone that is as hard as iron!' (333).

Twain is dismissive in a later notebook (kept during the 1878 European trip) of the 'gawking gangs of tourists [in St Mark's, Venice] poking about with red guidebooks [Murray] up to near-sighted eyes' (*NJ2*, 195–6). But he, too, relies heavily on such guides in all of his travel writing. And in the Holy Land, such reliance becomes especially noticeable. Twain can burlesque religious piety, the sentimental response to history and tradition and the value and importance of supposedly holy sites: nowhere more so than when he reports the 'touching' discovery of the 'grave of a blood relation', Adam, in Jerusalem, and weeps over it (567). However the comic tone quickly disappears when, soon after, he describes 'the place where the true cross stood', 'the last resting-place of the meek and lowly, the mild and gentle, Prince of Peace!' (573), at the Church of the Holy Sepulchre. There are some subjects Twain cannot joke about and the weight either of audience expectation or of his own conditioned response temporarily stifles the humour. A bumptious irreverence and an independent and iconoclastic voice drives the comedy forward in much of *Innocents Abroad*, but it is a more complicated and varied book than this. Its recognition of the necessary *inter*dependence of New and Old World cultures, of the continuing cultural weight of past readings of, and reactions to, that latter world, gives a peculiarly self-divided quality to the book, a quality that marks American identity itself.

But, to return to the Bellagio passage (201), there is one further thing to say here about the types of cultural movements occurring in the book. For travel is not just a matter of seeing American strengths and weaknesses anew in the light of European or near-Eastern comparison, nor of recognising the persistence of learnt and inherited responses to those older traditions and histories. There is also just the suggestion in that vision of a mixed-up 'mad panorama' that harasses Twain's 'brains', that both Old World and New lose their clear outlines, become strange and unfamiliar, when brought together and juxtaposed. There is a brief moment of genuine frisson in this calming vision/nightmare as he suggests just how radically disorienting and transformative transnational thinking and experience can be.[8] In Chapter 2, I described the sequence where the narrator's experience in Milan Cathedral (seeing a sculpture of a skinless man) triggers a sudden recollection of American childhood trauma. This is something of what I mean here – the way that present European experience throws the narrator off-balance and causes a momentary upsetting of the text's time scheme and of its spatial boundaries (with the move to a childhood Missouri past). As this happens, the narrator's very sense of himself, and the reader's view of him, is recast – briefly illuminated in a new and different way.

A Tramp Abroad

Twain's second European travel book, *A Tramp Abroad* (1880), did not have the immediate public impact of *Innocents Abroad*, but is a much better book than it is often given credit for. Among the things that made Twain's first travel books so distinctive were the mass of illustrations in the American Publishing Company's editions. As a subscription company, Twain's publisher depended on advance sales drummed up by its agents visiting the homes of potential buyers. Thus both the length of the book and the number of its illustrations (some of which would have been shown in the salesman's prospectus) were key sales factors. But what is also distinctive about these travel books is the narrative method Twain employs. He wanders, in an apparently improvised manner, from subject to subject. And he links these various movements through what Richard Bridgman calls 'mechanisms of association', as one topic provides some kind of trigger (a thought, a word, or an image) to call up its otherwise unrelated successor.[9] The narrative of the journey itself provides the loose and ongoing structure to a book that can then contain a miscellany of different subjects and modes of writing (description, anecdote, reminiscence, reported dialogue, commentary, etc). Moreover, much of the (sporadic) brilliance of the travel books lies in their alternating focus. At one moment, Mark Twain himself – or rather, the persona he adopts – is the subject of interest or spectacle. The next, the emphasis is on the environment, the countries he passes through and the sights that he sees.

Contrasting the traveller with the tourist in the discussion of *Innocents Abroad*, I indicated that the main protagonist, 'Mark Twain', belonged in the latter category. But the innovatory nature of the *Quaker City*'s voyage (as a pleasure trip to Europe and the Holy Land), and the strangeness and impact of many of its reported foreign sights, mean that the distinction cannot be kept entirely intact. In *A Tramp Abroad*, Twain is more self-consciously reflexive about mass travel and tourism. He pays more attention to the fact that the European countries he now visits, especially Switzerland (much of the book is set here, with another long first section in south-western Germany), are parts of a very well-worn tourist trail.

Mass tourism and Twain's own status as tourist, then, have even greater emphasis in this text than in *Innocents Abroad*. Here, he explicitly mocks the sensitive traveller – with her or his delicate awareness of the education to be gained from a foreign culture and its galleries, churches, buildings, museums, and inhabitants, and the elitist tendencies that accompany the separation from the general tourist mass. Indeed, Twain's description of the patronising young American, in Chapter 38, might be seen as a satiric nod in the direction of his contemporary, Henry James, well-known for his enthusiastic immersion in European culture and his aesthetic appreciation of its finest qualities. The American (twenty-three-year-old) 'adolescent' in *A Tramp Abroad* complacently contrasts himself with the surrounding 'herd'. He defines himself as 'a traveler – an inveterate traveler – a man of the world', and one who has an inti-mate knowledge of Europe and is 'a guest in the inner sanctuaries of palaces' there. He talks, too, of his visits to exquisite and out-of-the-way places: for example, to 'some forgotten castle [to worship] some little gem of art . . . which the unexperienced would despise' (440–3).

Twain, on the other hand, presents himself (especially in Switzerland) as one of a 'procession' (440) of tourists. He and the others remake the foreign countries they visit to their own needs. (Thus today, for instance, Grenada has becomes synonymous with, and often reduced to, the Alhambra, and to 'gyp-sies' dancing the flamenco in hillside caves.) Tourism leads to the collapse of 'authenticity' in the making of the 'pre-packaged . . . wholly touristic place . . . trumped up, corrupted, commodified'.[10] So Twain shows how, in the Switzer-land of his day, this process is already well advanced. The road from Lucerne is packed with 'an unbroken procession of fruit pedlars and tourist carriages' and 'little peasant boys and girls offer[ing] . . . bouquets of wild flowers . . . for sale' (328). The Jungfrau Hotel in Interlaken ('one of those huge estab-lishments which the needs of modern travel have created in every attractive spot on the continent') has waitresses 'dressed in the quaint and comely cos-tume of the Swiss peasants' (340). On the Rigi-Kulm mountain Twain hears 'the famous Alpine *jodel* in it own native wilds' for the first time and hands the shepherd-boy performer a franc. By the end of the day, finding yodellers 'every ten minutes', Twain and his companion (Harris) hire 'the rest of [them], at a franc apiece, not to jodel any more'. As the narrator comments: 'There is somewhat too much of this jodling in the Alps' (289–90).

If the Swiss act out expected stereotypes to cater to the needs of their foreign visitors, so the landscape changes (with the appearance of new hotels and shops) to cater for them. Twain plays up, and enjoys, his own role as tourist as he makes his trip. He does what all the other tourists do. He goes to watch the sunrise on the Rigi-Kulm – though, in his often-repeated role as a comic inept, he oversleeps in his mountain-top hotel and mistakes the sunset horn-blow for its dawn equivalent. Consequently, he finds that it is he and Harris who form the spectacle, as they stand alone as dusk falls, half-dressed and wrapped in red blankets, on the tall scaffolding built for the sunrise view (296–300).

At Mont Blanc, Twain watches 'the gangs of excursionizing tourists arriving and departing with their mules and guides and porters' (512). But though he is happy to follow the tourist trail and enjoys the comfortable hotels and good meals on it, he is less willing than his fellows to make the physical efforts that are normally part of that process. Indeed one of the central jokes of the whole book rests on the way that Twain and Harris avoid even the basic form of (supposedly-pleasurable) exercise that gives the book its title, avoiding 'tramping' in favour of the taking of train, horse and carriage, or raft, whenever possible. So, rather than climb Mont Blanc, they join in the activity by proxy, following the progress of one party through a telescope from Chamonix, and raising a 'triumphant, tremendous shout' as – via that medium – they too reach the summit (512–20). Away from any strenuous mountain-side activity, Twain is happy to make all the normal tourist rounds. He describes the 'pretty little shops' in Geneva with their 'enticing gimcrackery' (541), the 'memento-factory' at the Mer de Glace (where he buys 'the usual paper-cutter to remember the place by, and had Mont Blanc [. . .] branded on my alpenstock', 539), and the 'bewildering array of Swiss carvings and the clamorous *hoo*-hooing of . . . cuckoo clocks' seductively displayed in Brienz (339).

In *A Tramp Abroad*, Twain engages issues that have since become central to the travel narrative. He shows how tourism affects, and promotes a false version of, the countries it colonises. He is aware, too, of the mutual part both guest and host play as this occurs, illustrating within the book his own (comic) part in this process. *Innocents Abroad* does do something of this same thing, but its treatment of the topic lacks the self-reflexive and sustained intensity of the later book. This intensity is encouraged by *A Tramp Abroad*'s different setting – for we should remember that the huge popularity of Chamonix in the nineteenth century, for instance, led to its being described by *Blackwood's* as a 'little London of the high Alps'.[11]

The two books contrast in other ways too. The 'Mark Twain' generally represented in *A Tramp Abroad* differs from the earlier persona. There are fine comic set pieces in the 1880 book, where the narrator displays a similar capacity for naïve misapprehension, lunatic mayhem, and ignorance and accident, to that shown in the earlier work (see for instance the 'Great French Duel,' 69–82; the 'Night Excursion,' 114–21; and the Alpine sunset sequence described above). Ethnocentric comedy is still used, too, but not nearly as insistently as in *Innocents*. Twain's humorous attack on 'The Awful German Language', has, nonetheless, become a classic of its kind and contains some memorable jokes: 'I heard a California student in Heidelberg, say . . . that he would rather decline two drinks than one German adjective' (606). Twain proves his mastery, in *A Tramp Abroad*, of the extended and apparently irrelevant anecdote. And here – at least in the case of Jim Baker's celebrated 'Blue-Jay Yarn' (38–42) – he confidently allows himself all the time and space he needs for its telling.

Twain is less cocksure here than he was in *Innocents Abroad*, less fiercely combative in his rejection of European cultural models. He still aims his barbs at European high art. Thus, seeing *King Lear* played in German, he reports that his party 'never understood anything but the thunder and lightning' (83). But he is now more willing to tone things down and to admit his own aesthetic inadequacies. This continues into his later work. In 'Down the Rhône' (1891), for instance, he accepts that an ability to appreciate the *Mona Lisa* depends on the taking of advice he had previously been given: 'you must train your eye – you must teach yourself to see' (*EE*, 144). The brash narrator of *Innocents* would have had no time for such counsel. Another difference in *A Tramp Abroad* is that we seem much closer in this text to the actual Mark Twain (Samuel Clemens), a well-established American author, making his comfortable way through Europe and reporting, sometimes humorously, sometimes relatively straightforwardly and seriously, on his experiences there. The fact that Twain travelled on this trip with his family – though this information is generally kept out of the book – and, briefly but crucially, with friend and minister Joe Twichell ('Harris'), may also help to explain this difference.

Again, this book's subject matter calls for a transnational reading. Twain's reports on Europe serve as an oblique commentary on the strengths and weaknesses of his home culture. And there is a significant difference between this travel book and its predecessor in the more critical view of America now revealed. Twain had made a trip to Bermuda in May 1877 (just under a year before the European travel on which *A Tramp Abroad* would be based), accompanied – in what served as a type of trial run for the later journey – by friend Twichell. In 'Some Rambling Notes of an Idle Excursion', the travel piece that reported on the Bermuda visit and later republished in *The Stolen White Elephant, Etc.* (1882), Twain celebrates the benefits of leaving America: of 'being free and idle, and of putting distance between ourselves and the mails and telegraphs' (36). He made a similar point, more strongly, in his notebook: 'Bermuda is free (at present) from the triple curse of railways, telegraphs, & newspapers' (*NJ2*, 36). In 'Rambling Notes' he goes on to describe the 'millions of harassed people' (40) in his own fast-modernising country, and the contrasting pleasure he finds in the 'pure recreation' (36) enjoyed in Bermuda. The tidy rural charms of the country and the easy racial harmony there are implicitly contrasted with the urban developments and the racial unease of the land he has just left (he has sailed from New York).

Twain's descriptions of the European landscape and way of life in *A Tramp Abroad* continue this veiled commentary on what he saw as developing faultlines in American culture. The 'Mark Twain' who appears in this text reveals clear signs of neuroticism and anxiety: he suffers from 'nervous excitement' as he tries to sleep (114) and describes himself as a 'nervous man' when discussing his 'pet aversion' to 'the distressing '*hoo*'hoo! *hoo*'hoo! *hoo*'hoo!" of the cuckoo clock (262). We should remember that in 1881 George Beard would publish his *American Nervousness* (a follow-up on his earlier *A Practical Treatise on Nervous Exhaustion*), which identified nervous exhaustion as a specifically

American disease – a product of modernisation and its associated technologies (see Twain's 'triple curse' above).

Twain shows, in *A Tramp Abroad*, his sharp awareness of the faults of a Europe lacking the comforts, material advantages and lack of superstition that have accompanied modernisation in America. He describes 'the packed and dirty tenements' (163) of the village of Hirschhorn in Germany and tells of the 'liquid "fertiliser"' that swamps the streets in the Swiss village of Leukerbad ('They ought to either pave that village or organise a ferry', 391). Jokes scatter the text about the prevalence of fleas in the hotels that he and Harris visit. At a late point in the book, too, Twain composes a richly sensual tribute to the deliciousness of American food and drink in comparison to European hotel food and its 'monotonous variety of *unstriking* dishes' (573).

But he is also aware of the different pace and mode of life in Europe and the advantages they bring. When he arrived in Frankfurt at the start of the trip, he wrote to Howells describing his 'deep, grateful, unutterable sense of being 'out of it all'' (*THL*, 227). From Heidelberg, he continued in a similar vein: 'Lord, how blessed is the repose, the tranquillity of this place! . . . It is so healing to the spirit' (230). Repeated descriptions in *A Tramp Abroad* confirm this sense of a welcome escape from the pressures of American modernity, nowhere more so than in the account of the Neckar raft trip (in many ways a rehearsal for the more sustained focus on this form of river travel in *Huckleberry Finn*). On the raft, Twain enjoys the 'gentle, and gliding, and smooth, and noiseless' motion, that 'calms down all feverish activities,' and which is so different from the 'dusty and deafening railroad rush' (126) of the modern land-transportation system. The Black Forest (in Germany) is also valued for the 'remoteness of the work-day world' found there, and the consequent sense of 'entire emancipation from it and its affairs'. A 'suggestion of mystery and the supernatural . . . haunts' this landscape, lending it something of a religious atmosphere: 'a rich cathedral gloom pervades the pillared aisles' (207–8).

Twain's leisure trip in Europe, going where and when he pleases, in the easy companionship of a good male friend, becomes, then, a way of signalling his dissatisfaction with modernity and the bustling post-bellum American civilisation that primarily represents it. The illustration, 'The Author's Memories', on the opening page of the main body of the text (16) shows an apparently harassed Mark Twain busily writing. A large basket full of (discarded?) manuscript pages and a huge pair of scissors (for cutting and pasting?) are at hand, with other travel books – no doubt to consult and borrow from – on the floor. The circle of images (boat, raft, village, duel, castle, village, mountains, horse and carriage etc.) surrounding the author – rising in a cloud of smoke from a large pipe – gives the impression of dizzying activity (and we know Twain found this book

The exuberance of the book is in part a product of the new environment and social world Twain represents. The stagecoach travelling West is a womb-like space, with its human cargo stripped to their underclothes, with its curtained interior (in the conductor's graphic words) 'dark as the inside of a cow' (37). Eastern clothes are left behind, soon replaced by 'slouch hat, blue woolen shirt and pants crammed into boot-tops' (168). The heavy U.S. Statutes and Unabridged Dictionary Twain and his brother carry turn out to be only a nuisance (38–9) in a world where the normal legal and verbal rules just do not apply. Twain addresses the silent woman who boards the stage-coach early on with the observation that 'The mosquitoes are pretty bad, about here, madam'. Her answer – 'You bet!' – throws him off track and leads to his own more elaborate reply: 'What did I understand you to say, madam?'

Standard American English and grammatical correctness are clearly inappropriate, stiff and over-formal, here. But, at the same time, the linguistic inventiveness and colloquial forms of expression of this new Western world (as represented in the woman's voice) are themselves implicitly criticised by the narrator, in what is then shown as the monologic and bludgeoning manner of their delivery. Despite this, the non-stop stream of (for the reader) gloriously comic and highly expressive language that the woman speaks suggests the creative possibilities and vigour of a different form of American English. For her words are grounded in the vernacular, and startlingly different from the expected Eastern norm: 'Danged if I didn't begin to think you fellers was deef and dumb. I did, b' gosh. Here I've sot, and sot, and sot, a-bust'n muskeeters and wonderin' what was ailin' ye. . . . I begin to reckon you was a passel of sickly fools that couldn't think of nothing to say' (27). The brilliant later exchange between the 'stalwart rough', Scotty Briggs and the 'fragile . . . new fledgling from an Eastern theological seminary' (the Buck Fanshaw's Funeral sequence) repeats this clash of different speech registers. This episode again illustrates the forceful energy of the Western vernacular but also refuses to privilege a Western language and value scheme over its Eastern counterpart (even as Twain satirises the over-formal and genteel qualities of that latter voice) (see 329–38). For one of the markers of this book, and of other Twain texts too, is the author's relativism: his tendency to set different ways of life and ideological positions against one another without necessarily choosing between them.

Twain's imagination is, however, clearly engaged and stimulated (if often confused) by this new and different Western world. The narrative appears to chart a progression from tenderfoot to fully-fledged Westerner. Twain, at first, is repeatedly taken in by the hoaxes and practical jokes of the community he looks to enter. He is totally persuaded by the seeming 'guileless candor and truthfulness' of the man who advises him on the qualities of 'a Genuine

Mexican Plug' in Carson City when he looks to buy a horse at auction (the man turns out to be the auctioneer's brother), even though he has not a clue what a Mexican Plug is. The horse, unsurprisingly, turns out to be completely unhandleable. When another rider (who can at least stay on his back) borrows him, the horse pulls to a halt 'with one final skip over a wheelbarrow and a Chinaman'. Twain finally gives him 'to a passing Arkansas emigrant whom fortune delivered into my hand' (178–84).

Twain eventually becomes part of the community about him, initiated into the ways of Western life. At the same time, however, there is a repeated sense of frustration, of bright promise and succeeding disappointment, as he attempts to fulfil himself in this new world. The 'blind lead' episode – where he and Higbie, a fellow miner, discover the existence of an unsuspected vein of ore-rich rock, but then (for various reasons) fail to work it within the regulated period and thus lose a promised fortune (277–91) – is paradigmatic in this respect. Twain describes this incident as a 'curious episode' in 'my slothful, valueless, heedless career' (277), words that cut against any real notion of development and growth. Indeed, he moves in the narrative from one place to another, all of which finally prove, in one respect or another, to be unsatisfactory.

Hawaii (which he visits as tourist and reporter acting on behalf of American commercial interests) is the last point westward on Twain's journey. After this, he returns to San Francisco and then back East, in the direction from which he first came. The dream-like atmosphere in Hawaii (with its 'dusky native women' and its 'Summer calm as tranquil as dawn in the Garden of Eden') is interrupted by a 'scorpion bite' (456–7). This aptly illustrates the pattern of idyllic expectation and painful reality that recurs throughout the book. Twain, too, constantly changes occupation and profession. The question at the start of Chapter 42 – 'What to do next?' – suggests the overall sense of uncertainty in his story and its lack of final resolution. Twain does end up as the successful performer of comic lectures – and this was a career he would (in reality) follow, one closely related to his profession as a writer. But the conclusion of the book undermines any sense of positive resolution and development to his narrative. For it ends with yet another practical joke (with Twain as its butt), and with a 'moral' that partly reads, 'If you are of any account, stay at home and make your way by faithful diligence' (570).

The initial sense of promise and adventure with which the book starts, and the largely unwritten territory that Twain travels does, however, seem to have liberated him in certain ways as a writer. For the book is full of extended anecdotes, tall tales and digressions. Twain seems more willing to take his time and to interrupt the flow of the narrative than he was in *The Innocents Abroad*. So in Chapter 53, to take one striking example, Twain tells how 'the boys' in Virginia City repeatedly suggest that he gets 'one Jim Blaine to tell me the stirring story of his grandfather's old ram', but insist that Blaine needs to be drunk before he should ask. Eventually this condition is met and Blaine tells his story. This is a brilliant comic performance on the author's part. Blaine, rather like Simon Wheeler in 'Jumping Frog', wanders from one reminiscence to another. As this happens, the apparent main subject of the story is left completely behind, only mentioned in his opening remark: 'There never was a more bullier old ram than what he was. Grandfather fetched him from Illinois'. Twain, as he finally finds out, has been 'sold', for Blaine always 'maunder[s] off' in the way he now does and has never been known to finish his tale. More, as he tells it, he is oblivious to everything except the details of the people, places and incidents he recalls, completely locked in a solipsistic narrative world.

This whole story (or rather series of stories connected by the slimmest of interconnecting narrative 'triggers') contains many comic highlights. Two in particular stand out. The first recounts information about Miss Jefferson's glass eye. Miss Jefferson enters the tale when a drunk is 'scooted', by the officiating deacon, through the window of a room where a church-meeting is being held, 'and he lit on old Miss Jefferson's head, poor old filly'. The story continues (I quote selectively here):

> She was a good soul – had a glass eye and used to lend it to old Miss Wagner, that hadn't any, to receive company in; it warn't big enough, and when Miss Wagner warn't noticing, it would get twisted around in the socket, and look up, maybe, or out to one side, and every which way, while t'other was looking as straight ahead as a spy-glass. Grown people didn't mind it, but it most always made the children cry, it was so sort of scary. She tried packing it in raw cotton, but it wouldn't work, somehow – the cotton would get loose and stick out and look so kind of awful that the children couldn't stand it no way. She was always dropping it out, and turning up her old dead-light on the company empty. . . .

The second is the description of William Wheeler, who was:

> nipped by the machinery in a carpet factory and went through in less than a quarter of a minute; his widder bought the piece of carpet that had his remains wove in. . . . There was fourteen yards in the piece. She wouldn't let them roll him up, but planted him just so – full length. . . . They didn't bury him – they planted one end, and let him stand up, same as a monument. And they nailed a sign on it, and put – put on – put on it – sacred to the – m-e-m-o-r-y – of fourteen y-a-r-d-s – of three-ply – car – pet – containing all that was – m-o-r-t-a-l – of – of – W-i-l-l-i-a-m – W-h-e –.

At which point Blaine falls asleep, 'the boys', meanwhile, 'suffocating with suppressed laughter' (383–90).

Blaine's monologue (from which these are only extracts) is brilliantly told as Twain shows his absolute control of, and feeling for, the vernacular voice. His ability to represent an apparently endless (till the drink takes effect) and meandering narrative in so few pages of text is extraordinary. The comedy relies in part on the violence and grotesquerie of western folk humour, but his ability to layer narrative detail on detail, to increase its effect, lifts this far above the normal level of the form. So, too, does the figurative language and modes of expression he uses ('straight ahead as a spy-glass', 'dead-light'). The thematic content of the stories (the gap between inner being and outward appearance, the sensitivities of children, the relation between industrial machine and human subject) may not reverberate strongly, but the visual quality of the humour and the sheer economy and effectiveness of its presentation show Twain at his comic best. There is moreover something self-reflexive here. Blaine's own associative technique (one subject prompting another) and the way that lots of small (metaphorical) nuggets of narrative gold are picked from the ground of his memory to be combined to such entertaining effect, provide a condensed and comedic version of Twain's own less intensive and more coherent structural and narrative tools.

But there is also something in this book that is reminiscent of Twain's European travel books. A dream of individual freedom and autonomy haunts the text. Twain originally sets out, leaving 'years [of] . . . toiling and slaving' in the 'close, hot city' behind, with 'an exhilarating sense of emancipation from all sorts of cares and responsibilities' (25). Once West – and feeling 'rowdyish and "bully"' – he writes that 'nothing could be so fine and so romantic' (168). At Lake Tahoe, in air that 'angels breathe' (170), he and his companion lead a life of 'luxurious rest and indolence' (174), masters of the land they have claimed and completely at one with their surrounding world. 'If there is any life' he states, 'that is happier than the life we led on our timber ranch for the next two or three weeks, it must be a sort of life which I have not read of in books' (173). Twain's own book is in many ways a celebration of the West and the self-fulfilment to be found there. In particular, it is an elegy for the 'old mining regions of California', and a way of life now (at the time of writing) vanished: 'an assemblage of two hundred thousand *young* men – . . . stalwart, muscular, dauntless young braves, . . . a peerless and magnificent manhood' (415).

But there is a tension and paradox in Twain's view of the West and the 'manhood' he celebrates that recurs elsewhere in his writing. For free spaces, idyllic interludes and autonomous male self-hood are all highly qualified here:

places and states of being which exist, but the fragility and temporary nature of which are fully and clearly recognised. Twain's idyll at Tahoe is destroyed by his own hand, as a fire he lights gets out of control. And, in any case, he is there for business ends, to start a timber ranch – for the mining industry nearby depended on vast quantities of timber for its very existence and there is already 'a saw-mill and some workmen' (170) just three miles from the spot. Twain celebrates the early gold-mining days and the energy and gallantry of its male population. But his description starts with a reference to the disfigurement of the landscape by 'avaricious spoilers', and ends with his mourning the disappearance of this population, apparently due to the materialist frenzy that prompted its first presence ('all gone, or nearly all – victims devoted upon the altar of the golden calf', 414–15).

Thus the promise of idyllic freedom is immediately compromised by the commercial activities which have drawn its inhabitants to that place, and the vigour of the population carries the seeds of its own demise in the greed that drives it. There is more to it than this, though. For Twain makes clear that any way of looking at America that ultimately tries to separate out East from West and individual freedom from corporate development is a type of false consciousness (a false consciousness, it has to be said, that underlies much of the tensions within a larger American ideology).

In his European travel books, Twain shows that America and Europe have what are, in many ways, interdependent histories and cultures. So, here, he suggests that there are firm connections that bind the American regions (in this case East and West) and make them together part of one greater commercial whole. Moreover, there is little part for a romantic individualism in this larger picture. As the mining industry grew, so necessarily, the vast percentage of its profits relied on the type of technology that only corporate wealth and its organisational structures could fund and run. Twain's description of the Gould and Curry mine in Virginia City talks of labouring men and their wages, and how 'they worked in three "shifts" or gangs . . . blasting and picking and shoveling' twenty-four hours a day (303, and see 378–9). He speaks too of the 'monster hundred-stamp mill' (312) the same company was erecting at near a million dollar cost. The future of the mining industry, in other words, whatever its wild-cat beginnings and traditions, lay in a mode of operation close to the factory system and wage-slavery back East.

The West became ever-closer in travelling time to the East as the inter-continental railway-system was built (see, for instance, 46–7). The telegraph already gave near-instantaneous communication across the continent. San Francisco's status as a financial centre was in considerable part dependent on the nearby presence of the Comstock Lode – which also stimulated a range of new technological development and 'elevated mining into the company of America's biggest businesses'.[15] Twain's account of Nevada mining practices, and particularly the feverish buying and selling of stock he describes, mirrors the activity in the commodities markets back in Chicago and New York. The whole American financial system at the time depended on western mining and the amount of gold and silver in circulation. Twain writes himself into the West only to reveal (though in a partial and incomplete manner) that he has written himself back into the economic and social complexities his younger self had thought to escape. For the West he describes was already incorporated, or fast-becoming so: part and parcel of an emergent capitalist national whole.

Life on the Mississippi

The ambiguous relationship between the sense of romantic male autonomy and the developmental logic of capitalism found in *Roughing It* is repeated in *Life on the Mississippi*. In the earlier text, what initially seems a clear difference between Western freedom and the constraints of Eastern life becomes more problematic on closer analysis. And this is also the case in *Life on the Mississippi* – where a similar tension is replayed in Twain's descriptions of river life before and after the Civil War. In both books, in fact, the seeds of the corporate American present are discoverable in preceding conditions and, in the case of *Life on the Mississippi*, despite the sharp historical rupture that had since occurred. Something of this pattern will also emerge in later discussion of *The Adventures of Tom Sawyer*.

Despite some first-rate sequences, *Life on the Mississippi* is not one of Twain's most successful books. It commenced as a series of 1875 reminiscences of Twain's apprentice piloting years for Howells's *Atlantic Monthly*. Titled 'Old Times on the Mississippi', this early material is repeated in Chapters 4 to 17 of the eventual published book. When this memoir first appeared, Howells responded to the episodes he received with words like 'capital' and 'extraordinarily good' (*THL*, 42, 59) and emphasised Twain's work of historical reconstruction: '*All* that belongs with old river life is novel and is now mostly historical' (46). Much of the later complete book would focus specifically on this sense of vanished history. Twain, revisiting the river in 1882, describes what he now sees on his travels down (and up) it, and contrasts present with past conditions.

There are plenty of strong chapters and episodes in the book and passages of considerable interest to any thematic study of Twain. The early sequence drawn from *Huckleberry Finn* (and not then replaced in its first published edition) offers a fine example both of Twain's comedy and of 'keelboat talk and manners'

(40–61), the life of an earlier form of river commerce. Twain then recalls (as in *Roughing It*) his own earlier self as he turns to autobiography and describes his apprenticeship to Horace Bixby as a Mississippi river pilot and the trials and tribulations of learning the river. It is this apprenticeship that gives the structural spine and comic grounding to the early parts of the book, as Twain again constructs his younger self as a naïve greenhorn and charts his education. One comic incident stands out, where Bixby, testing the confidence of his 'cub' in his new-found skills, has the boat's leadsman call shallower and shallower soundings as Twain pilots the boat over what, in reality, is a clear river crossing. Rather than trusting in his own knowledge of the river, Twain finally panics and shouts to the engineer: 'Oh, Ben, if you love me, *back* her! Quick, Ben! Oh, back the immortal *soul* out of her!' (164). He is accordingly humiliated before a watching audience. When the training is complete and the protagonist emerges as a 'full fledged' (246) pilot, however, this tool for organising the narrative is necessarily abandoned.

There are powerful descriptions in the book's early section of the stirring impact of the arrival of the steamboat on the otherwise sleepy little riverside town of Twain's boyhood. The author also recounts much of the business of river-boating as it existed at its commercial peak. Adding a very sombre note to what is generally a light-hearted account, he also includes a group of chapters (18 to 20) that describe his clash with the tyrannical pilot, Mr. Brown, and the death of his younger brother, Henry, in a steam-boat explosion which occurs just afterwards. Twain is remarkably reticent here about the emotions he himself felt at this time, though it is clear from other writing how much personal responsibility he (mistakenly) took for this death and how much it haunted him.

Twain proceeds from this earlier set of recollections to describe, from Chapter 22 onward, the river after the Civil War and the huge changes that have taken place. He tells how the growth of the railroad system and the increased use of towing-fleets (six or seven boatloads of goods) for freight have 'killed the steamboat passenger traffic' (256) more or less stone dead. The structural spine of the book is, though, broken with the change from the colourful and often nostalgic reminiscence of the pre-war days to a narrative of present-day travel on the river, with little sense of 'Mark Twain' as a constructed comic persona remaining. What replaces him is a by-and-large serious-minded author describing what he sees and what has changed, adding the odd anecdote and comic story as he goes. It may well have been that Twain's contemporary audience, wanting to know more about the country in which they lived and its changing social and industrial base, appreciated his work here. It may also be that the author himself was determined to record a vanishing history before it completely disappeared. But to a modern audience the many facts, statistics and descriptive passages introduced are out of kilter with the kind of writing they expect from Twain's pen. They tend to overwhelm the book's many other exceptional and often comic, parts.

As he re-travelled the river, so Twain briefly commented on the Civil War and the changes it had brought. By and large, though, and unsurprisingly given the times, he is careful not to offend the sensibilities of his readers, Southern or Northern. Battles are mentioned and the experiences of those who were involved in them are described. But when, for example he mentions the 'memorable' Fort Pillow massacre, Twain does not give any pertinent detail – that the Confederates committed a number of atrocities, including killing many Union soldiers and burying Negro soldiers alive, after the Fort had surrendered. Instead, he merely comments on the rarity of such massacres in American history (311). Twain may avoid here any direct engagement with unpleasant social realities. He does, however, anticipate William Faulkner in recognising how southerners would obsessively return to the matter of the Civil War ('The war is the chief topic of conversation') and the way it became the chief benchmark of southern history and experience: 'In the South, the war is what A.D. is elsewhere: they date from it' (454).

Similarly, Twain's approach to race, still an explosive subject at this time, is muted in this book. He describes how Murel (John A. Murrell, one of the South's most notorious outlaws) took repeated illegal financial advantage of the status of slaves as property and how he would then murder these 'poor wretches'. But this conduct is seen clearly as completely outside the scan of normal racial practice (311–15). He does explain the new patterns of migrant life of a black population no longer bound through slavery to one master and location (326). But when he discusses a scheme aimed to regenerate agricultural life in the South (the Calhoun Company) it is noticeable that it is one that kept existing racial hierarchies ('planter' and 'former slave') firmly in place (365–8). Twain, then, is generally conservative on race matters in this book – when the topic is raised at all. And he also shows a tendency on occasion to slip into the stereotypes of minstrelsy in his representation of African Americans (see, for instance, the 'Skylark' anecdote, 327–8).

Where Twain does attack the South is in a less contentious area, (famously) for 'the debilitating influence' of the books of Sir Walter Scott. He claims that Scott, and the 'grotesque "chivalry" doings and romantic juvenilities' of his heroes, lie behind the 'inflated language' and 'other windy humbuggeries' still to be found in the region (416–17). 'Sir Walter,' Twain continues, 'had so large a hand in making Southern character, as it existed before the war, that he is in great measure responsible for the war.' He 'created rank and caste down there', forming a society 'in love with dreams and phantoms; . . . with the sillinesses and emptinesses, sham grandeurs . . . and sham chivalries of a brainless and worthless long-vanished society' (467–9). Twain also notes the idealisation of a pure Southern womanhood accompanying such romance (see, for example, 418–19 and 460–2), and that had – as Katherine Anne Porter was later to show – such a pernicious and long-term influence on women and their role in the region. If Twain makes his points with hyperbolic relish, there is an underlying truth to his charges.

Opposed to Scott and his nostalgic medievalism, Twain holds up the 'wholesome and practical nineteenth-century smell of cotton-factories and locomotives' (416) for admiration. And part of the story he tells in the book is of a post-bellum America, pragmatic and technologically progressive. This new spirit of 'progress, energy, prosperity' (254) is predominantly associated with the section of the Mississippi from St Louis northward. But it is when Twain reaches the upper-river towns that the celebratory note gets loudest: 'In Burlington [Iowa] . . . one breathes a go-ahead atmosphere which tastes good in the nostrils.' He then charts the 'surprise and respect' he feels as his boat 'plows deeper and deeper into the great and populous Northwest':

> Such a people, and such achievements as theirs, compel homage. This is
> an independent race . . . educated and enlightened; they read, they keep
> abreast of the best and newest thought; they fortify every weak place
> in their land with a school, a college, a library, and a newspaper; and
> they live under law. Solicitude for the future of a race like this is not in
> order.   (562–5)

This, however, is where we recall Twain's earlier travel books. For in *A Tramp Abroad*, Twain takes quite a different approach in his implicit critique of American modernity. And in *Roughing It*, he celebrates romantic individualism even as he charts the conditions that, from an early historical stage, will render it redundant. There are similar tensions and contradictions in *Life on the Mississippi*. Twain criticises much about the Old South and particularly the Walter Scott syndrome, a 'maudlin Middle-Age romanticism' (417) that lingers on even after the War. But he himself romanticises the river pilot. For as he put it, in his well-known description:

> a pilot, in those [pre-war] days, was the only unfettered and entirely
> independent human being that lived in the earth. . . . [E]very man and
> woman and child has a master, and worries and frets in servitude; but in
> the day I write of, the Mississippi pilot had *none*. . . . So here was the
> novelty of a king without a keeper, an absolute monarch who was
> absolute in sober truth and not by a fiction of words.   (166–7)

This is powerful and heartfelt writing and the words suggest Twain's own deep ambivalence about the progress he would celebrate later in the book and his own attraction to romantic forms. Twain is stretched in two incompatible directions here. Positive about the future, he looks longingly to the past. But his view of that river-boating past is itself problematic. For the steamboat traffic was itself an often fiercely competitive and corporate *business*: an industry whose 'itineries commodif[ied] and routinis[ed] travel on the Mississippi'.[16] And the 'romance of the free self' was, in such a context, an untenable notion.[17]

Twain's own discussion of the monopolistic practices of the pilot's association, as it looked to protect its members' economic interests against those of the boat-owners and captains, may look back to earlier forms of craft guild practice.[18] But it also foreshadows the systemic practices of modern industrial relations, and any notion of individual 'independence' disappears in such (essentially unionised) group activity. Moreover, as one critic points out, the 'daily drill[ing]' (155) to which the pilot's amazing memory is subject, 'comes to look uncannily like that extreme development of a specialised bodily function produced by techniques of industrial mass production spreading across America.'[19] Again, as in *Roughing It*, what we see here is a nostalgic glance back to prior notions of agency and freedom, but a retrospect which – even as it is made – offers early evidence of the conditioning power of a burgeoning modern industrial capitalist system.

Twain justifiably has it both ways here (and similarly in his book about the West). For there is in fact a large gap between the failure to exercise complete autonomy and in becoming just another cog among many in a dehumanising industrial system. If the notion of romantic self-realisation is incompatible with the reality of a confining socio-economic conditioning, there is a way out of the double-bind. *Elements* of pleasure and *degrees* of expressive freedom can be found even within a constraining business world, especially in the early stages of its development and can differ considerably in their extent. There is, however, always a tendency to find 'freedom' at exactly the place where we no longer are. Twain depicts keel-boating (made redundant by the steamboat) as a lost form of primitive but vital life, with its 'reckless . . . [and] profane', but still 'brave . . . honest, trustworthy . . . [and] picturesquely magnaminous' crews (41). Similarly, the 'flushest and widest-awake [Mississippi] epoch' (25) that steam-boating fostered was brought to a standstill by the outbreak of war and the development of the railroad. The railroad steam-engine, in its turn, was then to become an object of nostalgic affection in the electric age. Yet all three modes of transport finally function under the same 'sign of capital', and the inevitable economic change and growth it speaks of.[20] Nostalgia and modernity, free self-expression and constraint may be the twinned poles of Twain's work (and perhaps of American ideology as a whole) but the two are bound in symbiotic connection. It is the nature of that bond and the paradoxical relationship between the two sets of terms, which are of ongoing concern in Twain's works.

Tom Sawyer and *Huckleberry Finn*

In a late sequence in *Life on the Mississippi*, Twain returns to Hannibal, Missouri and tells of his first extended visit to his boyhood town for twenty-nine years. Climbing Holliday's Hill (the fictionalised Cardiff Hill of *Tom Sawyer*) and 'a good deal moved' by his recollections of the past, Twain writes that 'the things about me and before me . . . convinced that I was a boy again, and that I had simply been dreaming an unusually long dream'. His reflections on the immediate present, however – that he might, for instance, enter a house to find 'a grandmother who was a plump young bride' when he was last there – 'spoil' this illusion. The curious mixture here of 'the familiar and the strange' (524), much seeming the same but with a profound change occurred, would become an increasingly powerful motif in Twain's life and writings (especially in his later years). So, too, would the related sense of the instability of the boundary between reality and dream.

It was clear that this return to Hannibal had a considerable impact on Twain. He celebrates the beauty of the river view, 'one of the most beautiful on the Mississippi'. This outlook, unlike the faces of those around him 'scarred with the campaigns of life', 'had suffered no change; it was as young and fresh and comely and gracious as ever it had been' (525). He also recalls the people, events and emotions of that boyhood time. He remembers his own religious terrors of harsh and lasting punishment for bad behaviour: that he would share a similar fate to Lem Hackett, a boy who fell from an empty flat-boat and 'being loaded with sin, . . . went to the [river] bottom like an anvil' (530). He remembers, too, another death, that of the German boy 'Dutchy', drowned while taking part in a diving game in which Twain was a participant. He tells how he himself had chosen the straw to dive for this missing boy, and had 'grasped a limp wrist which gave me no response' deep beneath the water (536). There are a number of similar reminiscences of childhood encounters with violent death in Twain's writing and it is difficult to know how seriously to take them. There is no doubt of his tendency to embroider and re-invent the facts of his early life (the story of his brother Henry's death, for instance, changed considerably over the years)[21]. It is likely, however, that he did see more than his fair share of violent death in this period and that it had a lasting effect on him. His fiction is certainly death-haunted.

Twain returns, in the *Life on the Mississippi* chapters, to his old Sunday School, now replaced by a new building, and feels a 'yearning wistfulness' as he contemplates 'so many years gone by' (538). He remembers a local cave, turned into a 'mausoleum' to house the body of the owner's daughter, 'put into a copper cylinder filled with alcohol' (547). (The fictional version of the cave serves as a temporary mausoleum for Indian Joe's body in *Tom Sawyer*.) He also recalls 'Jimmy Finn, the town drunkard', and another 'whisky-sodden tramp' who had burned to death in the local jail with matches he himself had provided: 'I saw that face . . . every night for a long time afterward; and I believed myself . . . guilty of the man's death' (549). He revisits his old house to find it occupied by 'colored folk'. He comments that 'at present rates, [they] are of no more value than I am; but in my time they would have been worth not less than five hundred dollars apiece' (537), but fails to elaborate on the implications or possible moral reverberations of that statement. Going back over these recollections (many of which are painful), Twain sums up: 'The happenings and the impressions of that time are burned into my memory, and the study of them entertains me as much now as they themselves distressed me then' (549). He would return to such memories, repeat (and alter) them, over the course of his lifetime. The movement traced here between terror, nostalgia and entertainment becomes part and parcel of the fictional and (professedly) non-fictional representations they would inspire.

Twain published 'Old Times on the Mississippi' in 1875, when *Tom Sawyer* was already underway. His 1882 river trip was followed by the resumption and completion of *Huckleberry Finn*, after a long gap in its composition. Renewed memories of boyhood and of life on the river, and his own return to the Mississippi, undoubtedly stimulated his creative imagination, and the writing of memoir, travel book and fiction were all parts of the result. Out of this mix came his best-known novels: those based on 'the Matter of Hannibal'.

The Adventures of Tom Sawyer

The Adventures of Tom Sawyer (1876) 'lays claim', in Lee Clark Mitchell's words, 'to being America's most popular novel'.[22] As the useful University of Virginia Twain web-site puts it:

> In *Tom Sawyer* generations of readers have found access not just to
> childhood as a realm of summertime adventures, but to a mythic 'once
> upon a time' in the national past, a place before the disruptions of

industrialization, urbanization and immigration that were already beginning to transform the face of America even when [Mark Twain's] novel first appeared.[23]

'Tom Sawyer's Island' at Disneyland, and the way the fence white-washing scene has passed into common memory, are signs (among many more) of the novel's continuing popular appeal.

Twain's previous travel books were in many ways what we might now call (following Tom Wolfe) a form of 'new journalism', texts in which the boundaries between the performing subject and the objects of his attention, and between fiction and non-fiction, were highly unstable. *Tom Sawyer*, though, was Twain's first single-authored novel. In many ways a very nostalgic book (as suggested above), the book is far more than this. Indeed, it may be that its tensions, paradoxes and ambiguities – in many ways reflecting similar patterns in the minds of its readers – help to account for its 'classic' status. First written for adults, Twain was persuaded by Howells and his wife Olivia that the final product was children's fiction. In fact, one of the book's strengths is its ability to appeal both to child and adult at one and the same time.

The fence Tom Sawyer is supposed to paint, as a punishment for 'play[ing] hookey' (19) and for the state of his clothes after a fight with a new-comer to the village, is thirty yards long and nine feet high (26). In the book's original illustration its height is less daunting, more typical of small-town norms and images. But the size of this barrier between domestic and public space is significant, for the book depends on a whole series of boundaries crossed. Thus we are taken, in one direction, from Aunt Polly's house, over that fence and outward, to the larger village and thence to Cardiff Hill: 'beyond the village and above it, . . . green with vegetation, . . . just far enough away to seem a Delectable Land, dreamy, reposeful, and inviting' (26). In another, we are led toward the Mississippi and the uninhabited Jackson's Island.

Fence and windows (through which Tom makes his recurrent exits) mark the boundary between an adult and boyhood world and between community rules and the lack of constraints beyond. Twain writes in the 1870's but sets his fiction in the south-western village of St Petersburg (modelled on Hannibal) during the ante bellum period ('thirty or forty years ago', ix). This step backward is crucial to the book's success. America modernised extremely rapidly during and after the Civil War and the social and economic transformations that took place were profoundly disorientating. Those changes, in turn, were accompanied by a variety of crises that (for many) caused both bewilderment and anxiety. So, for instance, the 1873 financial panic, triggered by the collapse of the Northern Pacific Railroad, began a five-year depression in the country, with six thousand businesses closing in 1874 alone. In 1875, a strike in the eastern Pennsylvania coal industry was followed by the hanging of twenty Irish immigrant members of the Molly Maguires (a labour organisation) for the supposed murder of mine-owners and their representatives. The 1877 railroad strike brought mass violence between classes, this time on a nationwide scale, bringing fears of the outbreak of a second Civil War. Twain's move back to the communal life of rural and ante bellum small-town America offered an imaginative escape from such massive and upsetting social change. But a further step back accompanied this, away from adulthood and back to boyhood (indeed, this was just one in a spate of boy-books written in the period). It is easy to see how this double move would appeal to the audience of its day – and how it continues to appeal to a contemporary audience for whom the rural and anti-modern still hold a considerable attraction.

Twain's look back to an earlier and simpler world does not itself, however, guarantee full self-expression or pleasure for its young protagonists. Indeed, in some ways, Tom is in a similar position to the tick that he keeps in his percussion-cap box, driven from one side of the school desk to the other as he and Joe Harper 'exercis[e] the prisoner' (73). For if the shaping of nineteenth-century American male identity has been seen in terms of a 'dialogue in action between the value of . . . two spheres' (domesticity and a boyhood 'alternate world'), that model exactly fits the case here.[24]

Punishment and discipline predominate in the home and within the other authority systems that function in St Petersburg, as Aunt Polly (and the other representatives of this social world) look to check Tom Sawyer's more disobedient and rebellious impulses. If Tom loves play, these authorities represent by and large the world of work. Tom 'was over the fence and gone' to avoid 'capture and punishment' by his aunt (34–5). She belts him, hits him 'sprawling on the floor', in response to his 'audacious mischief' (and if on this particular occasion he is blameless, it is an exception that proves the general rule) (37–8). Tom gets a 'tremendous whack' from the school-master when he is playing (with the tick) in class (74). He is switched until the master's arm is tired when, in excuse for late attendance, he says that he has 'stopped to talk with Huckleberry Finn' (68–9), the 'juvenile pariah of the village' (63). He gets 'the most merciless flaying that even Mr. Dobbins had ever administered' (165) when he accepts the blame for Becky Thatcher's tearing of the page of the teacher's 'Anatomy' book (with its suggestive illustration of 'a human figure, stark naked', 162). In line with traditional disciplinary methods, teacher and guardian use, on these occasions, surveillance and corporal punishment to enforce their own ways of seeing and being. Conformity, restraint and model citizenship are their intended ends.

Such methods bounce off Tom, however, and have no effect. He subverts the hard work ethic of the community whenever he can. He does this by avoidance techniques (as at school), or by trickery. He trades liquorice and marbles for the tickets that will gain him a Bible – tickets meant to be earned by 'the industry and application' of memorising its verses (46). And he cons his friends not only into the 'hard labor' (25) of white-washing Aunt Polly's fence, but into giving him their own treasured goods as payment for so doing. This leaves him ready to 'skylark' (27), to exercise the 'pure freedom' (28) seen as that labour's opposite (Tom's trick here is to make his peers believe that they are playing even as they perform his onerous job for him and to produce profit from the punishment he himself evades). In this period, a developing industrial capitalism brought with it a certain hardening of the ways in which human life was sectioned off into separate parts. Childhood was increasingly seen as an acceptable time of play, while adult life was firmly defined in terms of labour. Tom represents the play and pleasure principle writ large, one increasingly disappearing from the lives of the 'work-oriented men' of Twain's own time.[25] These divisions are indicated, though not yet firmly drawn, in the earlier historical time represented in *Tom Sawyer*. Indeed, one of Twain's achievements is to reveal the final instability of such child-adult oppositions (and of the spatial boundaries around which such oppositions cluster) in the St Petersburg community, in his depictions of grown-ups who are just as fond as Tom himself of performing and 'showing-off' (49).

Tom consistently disrupts adult routines – during the sermon, and on school 'Examinations' day – through his playful imagination, most notably, when he interrupts his own funeral. Assumed lost and drowned, he has been conducting his own forms of surveillance on the village from his Jackson's Island base and returns at the moment of most effective dramatic potential. Tom's play and pleasure, however, are most freely practised beyond St Petersburg's fences, on the margins of, and outside, this social space. He and Joe Harper act as Sherwood Forest outlaws in the 'green aisles of the forest' (82–3) on the summit of Cardiff Hill, in a 'dense wood' (79). Tom and Joe, temporarily at odds with girlfriend and mother respectively, and Huck (who is always a social outsider), go to Jackson's Island to be pirates.

The games the boys play tend to be socially conditioned, stimulated by Tom's reading habits in adventure, mystery and romance. But their setting – apart from the normal community spaces, especially on Jackson's Island and the Mississippi – gives them a utopian charge. When Tom wakes on his first morning on the Island he is aware of the 'delicious sense of repose and peace in the deep pervading calm and silence of the woods' (121). While, playing in the river, he, Joe and Huck whoop and prance, with 'frolic' and 'fun', 'shedding clothes as they went, until they were naked' (134–5). Civilisation, it must be said, is never far away here, and the boys are soon uncomfortable about their absence from home. But despite such ambiguities, the further the boys go from the village, the more chances they have for unrestrained play and pleasurable and idle loafing.

As I suggest, however, the boundaries in this book between ordered community routines and rituals and their playful upsetting of them lack complete stability. Tom's games are learned ones and the adults in the community often behave in a child-like way. Tom, moreover, brings his love of dramatic performance right into that community's heart as he interrupts the funeral and turns the mourners' 'anguished sobs' (146) to joy as he and the other boys march up the aisle. The celebration that takes place may be a mark of relief at this safe return, but it also an admission of the success and scale of Tom's play and plotting – an acceptance of their own status as the 'sold' victims of his joke (147). The inherent cruelty and thoughtlessness of his act is more or less brushed aside in the shared pleasure finally gained from his theatrical surprise. The spatial boundaries in the book seem to prepare us for a one-way symbolic movement from rigid and predetermined social conditioning to playful free expression, and something of this is true. But part of the charm of the book, a measure perhaps of the simpler times it represents, is the way the community too is affected by Tom's playful spirit; can join in the laughter at the socially disruptive and anti-authoritarian nature of his jokes.

There is a further level to the spatial patterning of the book, however, which relates to the representation of Indian Joe. Joe enters the novel not as part of its daylight, but of its midnight world, in an ancient graveyard 'about a mile and a half from the village' (86). This is one of the few references in the novel to the longer history of the village, while the setting, the time of night and the conditions ('dead stillness' except for the hooting of an owl, 87) all help transport the reader into melodrama and the Gothic mode. The story here is one of 'resurrectionists' (Indian Joe, Muff Potter and the young Dr Robinson) robbing a grave – presumably for the latter's medical reasons. If the Gothic can function to reveal the hidden secrets of the everyday world and to rupture conventional generic and conceptual boundaries, something of this happens here. The tone of the novel changes with the dark threat introduced by Indian Joe, the 'murderin' half-breed' (89). And the stable and idyllic aspects of small-town life ('the sun . . . beamed down upon the peaceful village like a benediction', 42) are replaced by unnatural and murderous events: the digging up of a corpse, and Joe's revenge killing of Dr Robinson (89–90). The space on the edge of the village here becomes a nightmare realm, the place of social upset and uncontrollable violence, rather than the place where free self-expression might be found. The two possibilities of what lies beyond the social (anarchy or freedom) are thus symbolically played out.

As other critics have pointed out, Indian Joe and Tom are curiously twinned figures, and represent different types of departure and rebellion from village norms.[26] If Tom plays at violence and 'mak[ing] people shudder' (80), Joe is the real thing. And Tom's romantic and sentimental relationship with Becky is nightmarishly shadowed in Joe's violent (and implicitly sexual) cruelty – seeking revenge on the Widow Douglas, he threatens to 'slit her nostrils . . . notch her ears like a sow . . . tie her to the bed' (223). Joe is the repository of all the traits that St Petersburg and its white citizenry would deny and reject. Like Tom, he is associated with the crossing of symbolic boundaries. His active, agile and violent body evades, too, the (more serious) disciplinary procedures of the community, springs 'for a window . . . and was gone!' (188) as his crime is revealed in the courthouse scene. He is the racial and moral 'other' of the text, but also an illustration of what might happen were Tom's anti-social and rebellious tendencies taken to their extreme ends. In Joe, Tom's liberating move beyond the limits of social regulation meets its dark opposite.

Tom and Joe are twinned too in the final *vertical* spatial move of the novel as both descend into the 'labyrinth underneath labyrinth' and uncharted spaces of McDougal's cave (220). The book takes on mythic dimensions as Tom and Joe briefly confront each other in this space. Becky's presence as the virginal and helpless young girl caught in what (seen in schematic terms) is this subterranean triangular relationship adds a further threatening note to the scene and to the community values ultimately at symbolic stake. Tom is lost, but Joe is at home in this dark realm, where he can evade detection beyond (like Tom earlier) the social and, in this case legal, authorities. What is, in many ways, the melodramatic climax of the book comes when Tom, looking to escape from the cave, finds a 'jumping-off place', and sees 'a human hand, holding a candle' beyond it. His 'glorious shout' is cut short by the realisation that the hand belongs to Indian Joe – Tom is 'paralyzed' and Joe takes to his heels (245).

Thus Tom and Joe, alone (for Becky does not see what occurs), come face to face, though with a fissure in the path between them. This symbolic confrontation is the turning point in the book's Gothic plot, for Indian Joe is never seen alive again. His body is rendered docile, his anti-social potential quashed, when Tom and Becky are recovering from their eventual escape from the cave. For 'the great Judge Thatcher' (49), the highest representative of legal and social authority in the novel, orders the cave's door to be 'sheathed with boiler iron . . . and triple locked' (251), to prevent other children getting lost in its depths. On Tom's recovery, Joe, the 'bloody-minded outcast' (253), is then found lying dead by the door. Unlike the earlier fences and windows, this spatial barrier cannot be crossed and the savage and unregenerate element in the community is accordingly obliterated. The sign and symbol of an encroaching industrial age (the boiler iron) renders Joe's renegade individualism null and void.

My exploration of the text's symbolic boundaries begins, perhaps, to suggest the final limitations of this book and why Twain turned from Tom to Huck as his next Mississippi valley protagonist. The author famously said to his friend, Howells, that 'I have finished the story & didn't take the chap [Tom] beyond boyhood. . . . If I went on, now, & took him into manhood, he would just be like all the one-horse men in literature & the reader would conceive a hearty contempt for him' (*THS*, 91). Finally, Tom is too much a part of his community – 'a sanctioned rebel'[27] – to allow Twain to develop his figure very far. I suggest earlier that Tom's association with playfulness and the free expression of self is linked to his move beyond village boundaries. But I also show the permeability of the boundaries Twain constructs. To put this another way, if industrial capitalism would separate childhood play from adult work, the inhabitants of both spheres finally share the same set of social assumptions. Thus, in this ante-bellum setting, adults can, to a certain degree, be playful. And, more importantly, Tom can share the values and ultimate ambitions of that adult group.

Tom is finally both a successful member of the community and a businessman in chrysalis form. He is one, we can imagine, who will go on to play a full part in the fast-emerging capitalist culture of the time. Tom (as the whitewash scene illustrates) is all enterprise, able to make a profit from limited resources and a dab hand at trade. And if he is duplicitous, 'a wily fraud' (50), in his dealings (in this case over the Bible tickets), the profits remain the same. Enterprise and an eye for the main chance were part and parcel of American business life of the 1830s under Andrew Jackson's presidency, and Tom fits well in that context. He ends up with a fortune. The fact that this is probably stolen or criminally-made money – from 'Murrel's gang' (205) – seems not to be an issue. Indeed, this may even signal a loose connection between Tom and the 'robber barons' of a later time: Gilded Age capitalists, entrepreneurs, and – in the popular imagination – thieves. Tom ends up as a traditional American success story, with a 'simply prodigious' income and his future mapped at the 'National military academy' and the 'best law school in the country' (269). The conventional shape of this narrative conclusion means that the rebellious elements in his boyhood nature are ultimately revealed as nothing *more* than play, just a stage in a larger process of social assimilation and success. If, to recall, male identity at the time was shaped by the move between two spheres, domesticity and a boyhood alternate world, Tom is the true product of such a dynamic: ready – once his childhood is over – to take his place in the community as a 'one-horse' (because ultimately deeply conventional) American man.

Similarly, we might suggest that Twain's representation of ante-bellum American village life is – to take a resonant metaphor – something of a whitewash. We have learnt to be wary of projecting onto a foreign (in this case Indian) 'other' the deepest fears and anxieties of our communities, but this is exactly what happens in the case of Indian Joe in this novel, and his melodramatic representation. Joe is an 'Injun devil' (94) whose violence, cruelty, and suggested sexual threat are implied products of his racial difference. His neat disposal at the novel's end leaves the Hannibal populace intact and safe to continue their 'prosperous and happy' lives (275). This is a whitewash – for the suggestion is that Joe carries all the blemishes of this world and that any flaw in the St. Petersburg community is essentially minor, with nothing inherently to worry about. That vision is perhaps best indicated in the racial politics of the novel. For if the 'half-breed' Indian bears the shape of evil in the text, slavery – the institution on which the social hierarchies and (to an extent) the economy of such south-western villages as this were based – gets scarcely a mention here. In 'My First Lie and How I Got Out of It' (1899), Twain wrote that 'It would not be possible for a humane and intelligent person to invent a rational excuse for slavery' (*TSSE*, 440). Here, though, the institution stands unchallenged, completely side-lined in a more nostalgic and attractive version of antebellum life.

It is difficult not to like Tom Sawyer, an adventurous and free-spirited boy but one who will (it seems) ultimately conform to community codes, and indeed become a leader in that social world. Indeed, we tend to project similar roles onto ourselves and our children, as we choose to overlook the incompatibilities between the free expression of self and actual social restraint, and between the mythology of success and the realities of economy and class status. Similarly, it is still both tempting and attractive (both in America and beyond its boundaries) to imagine and nostalgically celebrate earlier forms of rural life: 'childhood-as-it-ought to-be in small-town America'.[28] If this is not quite the picture Twain presents us with, as he indicates (for instance) that the seeds of future economic patterns lie in the practices of that past world, it is the one that many readers retain. And Twain does mask here the deep racial problems that rendered such a social world deeply morally problematic. Given the way the author himself either fails to foreground or to resolve such ambiguities in his novel, it is unsurprising that generations of readers have failed to do so either. Indeed, it is exactly in such evasions and compromises, such failures to resolve ideological contradiction, that the book's ongoing success and popularity most probably lies.

Adventures of Huckleberry Finn

Adventures of Huckleberry Finn came out in America in 1885 (though published in Britain the previous year). Twain changes literary tack here, perhaps to escape the more conservative and conventional aspects of his previous St Petersburg book and to look, too, to resolve its stylistic unevenness. For *Tom Sawyer* does lack overall unity and coherence, both in terms of style and genre.[29] The third person narrative voice often uses a heightened and deeply conventional form of diction: '[Tom] sat down on a mossy spot under a spreading oak. There was not even a zephyr stirring' (79). Elsewhere, Twain satirises what he calls in the Examination day scene, the 'wasteful and opulent gush of 'fine language'' (171). Where the novel comes alive, though, is in the author's use of direct speech and the vernacular. Thus, for instance, when Dr Robinson has knocked out Muff Potter, Tom and Huck have the following exchange:

> '. . . . maybe that whack done for *him*!'
> 'No, 'taint likely, Tom. He had liquor in him; I could see that; and besides, he always has. Well when pap's full, you might take and belt him over the head with a church and you couldn't phase him. He says so, his own self.'   (94)

To generalise from this one example is to suggest Twain's remarkable talent for matching speech patterns to character type and to the class, age, race and background of his different protagonists.

In *Huckleberry Finn*, Twain plays on this strength when, in one of the most celebrated developments in the American literary history, he put his full-length novel into the control (and voice) of his first person narrator and protagonist, the ill-educated and low-class Huck Finn. It is easy nowadays to downplay the importance of Twain's innovatory use of the vernacular. But we should not forget just how radical and important a step this was. Hemingway may have been exaggerating when, in the opening chapter of *Green Hills of Africa* (1935), he said that 'All modern American literature comes from one book by Mark Twain called *Huckleberry Finn*. . . There was nothing before. There has been nothing as good since'. But his words nonetheless indicate just what a groundbreaking book this was.

In this novel Twain, despite all previous writing done in the vernacular mode, effectively shattered the accepted boundaries of literary language in America. Huck's opening words, 'You don't know about me, without you have read a book by the name of 'The Adventures of Tom Sawyer,' but that ain't no matter. That book was made by Mr Mark Twain, and he told the truth, mainly', are not syntactically correct ('without you have read', 'ain't no') and use slang forms ('ain't' for 'is not'). But, most importantly, they convey the *impression* of colloquial and vernacular expression without extreme distortion of either spelling or grammar. This is something at which Twain was just brilliant: representing ill-educated forms of speech in a way that was entirely accessible to a general readership.[30]

To measure his achievement we need only look at the opening of George W. Harris's 'Sicily Burns's Wedding', from his *Sut Lovingood. Yarns Spun by a Nat'ral Born Durn'd Fool* (1867). This was a book Twain re-read as he was writing his novel and which undoubtedly influenced him.[31] The start of Harris's 'Wedding' story displays the standard framing device of south-western humour, with the vernacular voice of Sut 'contained' by that of a clearly well-educated and grammatical first narrator. Twain would abandon such a device in his novel, alongside the superior (and conservative) value-scheme normally associated with such a narrator. But Harris's opening also illustrates the difficulty of reading a text that represents dialect language by means of an extreme distortion of grammar and spelling (very much the comic rule until Twain himself amended it):

> 'HEY GE-ORGE,' rang among the mountain slopes; and looking up to my left, I saw 'Sut,' tearing along down a steep point, heading me off . . . , holding his flask high above his head. . . .
> Whar am yu gwine? take a suck, hoss? This yere truck's *ole*. I kotch hit myse'f, hot this mornin frum the still wum. Nara durn'd bit ove strike-nine in hit – I put that ar piece ove burnt dried peach in myse'f tu gin hit color – better nur ole Bullen's plan: he puts in tan ooze, in what he sells, an' when that haint handy, he uses the red warter outen a pon' jis' below his barn; – makes a pow'ful natral color, but don't help the taste much. Then he correcks that wif red pepper; hits an orful mixtry, that whisky ole Bullen makes; no wonder he seed 'Hell-sarpints'.[32]

In his use of Huck's first person voice, Twain avoids such a dense and reader-unfriendly style, establishing an immediate intimacy with the reader, with the direct address to 'you' from the 'me' who writes, and with the easy colloquialism and throw-away manner of 'but that ain't no matter'. The reference, too, to the earlier *Tom Sawyer* seems unforced and unproblematic. Though to have the protagonist of a novel refer to his appearance in a prior fiction, and to the author of that work, is in fact immediately to put at risk any notion of realist transparency (the novel as reflection of life as actually lived). Moreover, it tends to draw attention to the hole in the central premise of the book: how could such an ill-educated boy possibly have an authorial role, and just when might the novel have been composed and written by him? But this is to nit-pick. The very success of the novel is measured in the way most readers suspend such potential disbelief as they are immersed into its events and their importance. Huck's reference to Mr Mark Twain telling the truth 'mainly' is sly – even while that 'Mr' implies a full respect for his status and profession. And it provides an effective introduction to a document whose young and (in many ways) naïve narrator seems outside the author's control and who appears to do little more than exactly and truthfully describe just what he sees and thinks as events take place.

In a likely response to his apparent dissatisfaction with the developing logic of *Tom Sawyer*, Twain radically reverses his literary approach in this novel. While Tom was a sanctioned rebel and finally belonged inside the community, sharing its values, Huck is an outsider. The only view we get of him in *Huckleberry Finn*, barring the illustrations, is from the inside (as his thoughts and actions are represented). But in *Tom Sawyer* he is described as 'idle, and lawless, and vulgar and bad', and as the village 'outcast' and 'pariah' (63–4). Partly redeemed from this last position as a result of his and Tom's actions in that earlier novel and the fortune that they find, Huck starts this novel uncomfortably poised within society, in the Widow Douglas's care.

But Huck is not at ease with this new domestic world and the Widow's disciplinary regime. In *Tom Sawyer*, he was distanced from Tom's conventional values, only finally lured away from a life lived in, and on, 'the woods, and the river, and hogsheads' by a type of blackmail ('we can't let you into the gang if you ain't respectable') (272). Once with the Widow, Huck is subject to a type of 'reformatory lovingness' as she looks to influence him to accept her and the surrounding society's, 'imperatives and norms'.[33] We see evidence of this when, for example, Huck tells us that: 'The widow she cried over me, and called me a poor lost lamb . . .' (18).

But Huck just does not understand much of her worldview, nor of the values she proposes, particularly their religious aspects. He responds accordingly:

> After supper, [the widow] got out her book and learned me about Moses and the Bulrushers; and I was in a sweat to find out all about him; but by-and-by she let it out that Moses had been dead a considerable long time; so then I didn't care no more about him; because I don't take no stock in dead people.   (18)

Twain relies here on his repeated and basic, but most effective, device, defamiliarisation or estrangement – what happens when a fixed and normative way of looking at the world meets (in this case) a narrator who is uncomprehendingly naïve. When Soviet critic, Mikhail Bakhtin describes this technique, he might have had Huck in mind: 'by his very uncomprehending presence . . . [he]

makes strange the world of social conventionality'.[34] Huck dismisses the worth of what is normally taken for granted – traditional religious education and Bible study and their lessons – since, he pragmatically judges, dead people (let alone long-dead people from the scriptures) can be of no use to him. The ironic twist here is that Miss Watson's story is of the freeing of the Hebrews from the oppression of slavery, but she herself remains blind to its relevance to her own position as a southerner and as a Christian. The reader's increasing perception of the hypocrisies, violence, and moral shortcomings of the society through which Huck passes comes about, in part, through such estrangements. It also, however, results from the representation of the African American male slave Jim, who belongs with Huck at the text's centre.

Twain's friend, Joseph Twichell, served as a young chaplain in the American Civil War. The letters he wrote back to his family provide a full and moving account of his experiences. Twichell was a strongly committed abolitionist but it is still noticeable that when he refers to the three servants he had during his army years, two are fully named, as Tim Gleason and Martin Furness, while the third is just 'Joe . . . a colored boy about twenty years old'.[35] Twichell's practice is normal for his time, but the contemporary reader is aware that in such naming lies the heritage of slavery and its denial of the full worth (and identity) of the African American. Twichell's Joe can become Twain's Jim with scarcely a beat lost, so any differences in individual African American character and experience can – by implication – also easily be overlooked. I am not accusing Twain or Twichell of racism (far from it) but I am pointing to Jim's name, and early identification only as 'Miss Watson's big nigger, named Jim', (22) as a mark of his less-than-human status in this slave-holding world. Such inferior status then becomes a legacy, as far as the African American's position in the larger nation goes, which would not be completely cast aside until much, much later. In *Tom Sawyer*, a footnote follows the mention of Mr Harbison's dog, 'Bull Harbison': 'If Mr. Harbison had owned a slave named Bull, Tom would have spoken of him as 'Harbison's Bull,' but a son or a dog of that name was 'Bull Harbison'' (96). The slave then is designated more clearly as owned property than even the family dog.

Tom Sawyer, to repeat, is a community insider. Huck and Jim, the two main protagonists of *Huckleberry Finn* are both 'outcasts' ('out-caste' in Jim's case). Whiteness is the accepted norm in *Tom Sawyer*, but it quickly takes on unpleasant connotations in *Hucklebery Finn* when it is explicitly identified with Pap Finn and his 'white' face, 'not like another man's white, but a white to make a body sick, a white to make a body's flesh crawl – a tree-toad white, a fish-belly white' (39). But in terms of the racial politics of the novel, Pap's 'whiteness' is exactly like any other southern man's, just a more extreme version of it.

The pairing of Huck and Jim, two outsiders – in flight from the authority of guardian and father, and owner, respectively – allows Twain to make the type of caustic and fundamental social critique that he could never have developed within the frame of *Tom Sawyer*.

There are many negative allusions to white southern values and behaviour in *Huckleberry Finn*. The Widow Douglas is associated with a 'stiflingly repressive ethic', while the Grangerfords and the Shepherdsons – who live according to the codes of southern and supposedly gentlemanly behaviour – are responsible for 'cold-blooded slaughter'. Pap himself is a figure of 'sheer brutality'. As one critic puts it:

> The way in which Pap is described . . . should alert any reader to the idea
> that, for Twain, the codes by which the dominant culture lives are
> inextricably linked to ideologies of race, even where his white
> protagonists are not slave-owners, or when no non-white characters are
> present in a particular episode.[36]

Twain, then, raises the ideological stakes here, writing a book that takes race and colour as its central subject. W. E. B. DuBois would later say that 'the problem of the Twentieth Century is the problem of the color-line'.[37] Twain, in *Huckleberry Finn*, took on and exposed that problem both in the context of antebellum slavery and of post-bellum prejudice and discriminatory racial practice.

In many ways, Huckleberry Finn departs considerably from Tom Sawyer. I have already spoken of Twain's use of a first person vernacular narration, but this book's stylistic differences go much deeper. In Tom Sawyer, the externalisation of evil in Indian Joe is the stuff of melodrama, as is his grisly end. In the more 'realistic' later novel, Twain tackles anew the issues of social belonging and exclusion, of social identity and of race. Huck is an outsider as Tom never is, but because of his race and youth he can move in and out of society as Indian Joe (Tom Sawyer's outsider figure) cannot. Where, earlier, evil was externalised in terms of a racially-threatening and violent 'other', here Twain turns from melodrama to a clear-eyed look at the social and moral fractures and failings that lie at the very heart of American life.

It will be useful to comment briefly here on the status of Huckleberry Finn as a realist text. Realist texts make a claim to transparency, appearing to offer a clear window outward onto the solid world they represent. Twain, accordingly, uses Huck, his first-person narrator, to provide a seemingly direct depiction of the world through which he moves.[38] The use of Huck's unmediated and lower-class voice allows Twain to produce a genuinely democratic art. The realist manifestos of his friend Howells would stress just such a requirement, though Howells's own lower-class voices are generally 'framed' by middle-class narrators and their values. Huck's voice, then, carries the reader 'transparently' through to the solidly-framed historical context he describes – that of small-town antebellum life and its bordering Mississippi environment. We are asked to take this regional and historical reality for granted, together with the range of social practices, racial distinctions, and cultural codes that compose it. Such assumptions, and the details that reinforce them, provide the realistic glue holding the whole novel in place.

But as my reference to Howells and his call for a democratic art form suggests, realism was defined in social and ethical, as well as aesthetic, terms in this period. The relationship between the human subject and the surrounding environment and the moral potential of that individual subject, were both very much at stake here. At the time (the 1880s), romantic beliefs in the authority and autonomy of the free and sovereign self – that the individual was in total command of her or his own fate – were no longer easily tenable. Realist texts, accordingly, emphasised the way their protagonists were embedded in and affected by, what we might call a 'thick' social context, and focused on such areas as dress, manners, occupations, community connections and beliefs, as ways of doing this. The closeness of the relationship between the individual and the material details and social practices that composed his everyday life lay at the very core of the genre (when defined within this framework).

Despite the increasing press of environment on character in the rapidly-changing post-bellum American world, realist authors still took the essential wholeness and coherence of the human subject for granted. Indeed, the genre is commonly described in terms of the balance it represents between the pressure of the environment on the individual and the ability of that individual still to act as a free moral agent despite the increasing complications and determining networks of that larger world.

Huckleberry Finn can work as a realist text according to such criteria. From such a standpoint, Huck is seen as a self-determining subject, a sympathetic and free-speaking young boy (in the sense, at any rate, that he speaks the text), making his way through a difficult world but retaining his integrity as he responds to it with a clear-seeing and pragmatic eye. Huck's decision to choose hell rather than to allow Jim back into Miss Watson's hands (for many critics, the climax of the book) can then be read – in realist terms – as an act of individual moral responsibility that counters any tendencies of the larger social environment to condition and shape his actions.

But there are other ways of approaching the book calling this reading into question. If we focus on plot rather than point of view, for example, such melodramatic episodes as the boarding of the Walter Scott and the hiding of gold in Peter Wilks's coffin, as well as the farcical shenanigans of the 'evasion' routine, signal a failure to conform to realist criteria. And at the ethical level, the possibility of escaping social determinants in independent moral action (Huck's decision) is deeply undermined by three things: by Miss Watson's prior actions (for Jim is in fact already freed); by Huck's passivity through-out the book (he is generally associated with spectatorship rather than action, and his main decision here is not to send the letter he has written); and by his consequent position as Tom Sawyer's helper, as Jim is placed in the role of victim to the boys' superior authority and power. The very idea of Huck as an intending and coherent subject is, moreover, interrogated by the extent to which his language and thought are inevitable products of the larger soci-ety that surrounds him, and by the textual emphasis on disguise and identity slippage (Huck recurrently adopts fake names and histories) which necessarily subverts any notion of fixed selfhood. Finally, and looking in an exactly opposite direction, the novel's debt to a Romantic tradition of unfettered individual-ism (the dream of free and autonomous selfhood which shadows the whole book and accounts for much of its mythic appeal) also undermines realist assumptions.

Where then does this all leave us? To sum up, Huckleberry Finn is gener-ally considered a realist novel, indeed one of the prime examples of Ameri-can nineteenth-century realism: this is not incorrect. But there are all kinds of instabilities within the text that call this realism into question. And if we look outward to other texts being produced at the time we see that this is not unusual – that realism, as considered as a particular generic movement of this time, cannot be seen as a coherent and unified genre. Caught between the romance, with its conception of the human subject as largely free from social determinants and naturalism (which, to state it crudely, sees the individual as conditioned and shaped by larger and uncontrollable forces) and continu-ing to rely on many of the plot devices and sentimentality of earlier fictional forms, realism is full of tensions and ambiguities stretching it in different, and often incompatible, directions. Twain's novel is entirely typical in this respect.

As part of his realist agenda, Howells celebrated the use of dialect in the novel, linking it to 'the impulse to get the whole of American life into our fiction'. 'Let fiction cease to lie about life', he wrote, 'let it speak the dialect, the language that most Americans know – the language of unaffected people everywhere'.[39] Indeed, it is in his extended and highly accomplished use of a variety of local dialects and its grounding in the details of everyday Mississippi valley life, that makes Twain, for many, the contemporary writer who best practiced what Howells preached. Huck's vernacular narration contains within it, and represents, all the other varied voices of his surrounding social world – those of Miss Watson, Jim, Buck Grangerford, Colonel Sherburn, the king and the duke, Aunt Sally and countless others. What Twain does so effectively here is to set Huck's voice in counterpoint with all these other voices.

If 'the power dynamics of society are determined by the language politics of education and literacy,'[40] then Huck has very little power in the world through which he moves. Miss Watson keeps 'pecking at' Huck (20), telling him how he should behave. The new judge determines who should be Huck's guardian (42), without Huck having any say in the matter. Colonel Grangerford, dressed in 'linen so white it hurt your eyes to look at it' and carrying his 'mahogany cane with a silver head to it' (143–4), regulates his small social world (his family, slaves, and – while he is there – Huck) with absolute authority: 'when . . . the lightning begun to flicker out from under his eyebrows you wanted to climb a tree first, and find out what the matter was afterwards' (144). Tom Sawyer, clearly well read, may be just a boy, but he manages the whole final evasion routine ('when a prisoner of style escapes, it's called an evasion', 337) according to the romance literature he loves. And he gives Huck little determining voice in the enacted events: 'he never paid no attention to me; went right on. It was his way when he'd got his plans set' (312).

But the power dynamics of Huck's world are not just organised according to language politics of literacy. Moving on the fringes of society, and passive by nature, he is pretty much at the mercy of anyone whose words claim power over him (at least, until he finds a way to escape them). Thus Pap, the lowest of the (white) social low, assumes a paternal right to order Huck about, and threatens to 'tan [him] good' should he carry on 'a-swelling [himself] up' by continuing to learn the literacy skills Pap himself lacks (40). The king and the duke, too, scoundrels and confidence men, or – in Huck's own words – 'beats and bummers' (242), take their authority over Huck (and Jim) for granted. As the king snaps at Huck: 'keep your head shet, and mind y'r own affairs – if you got any' (237). Huck does find his own methods of escaping and opposing such authority figures, but in terms of direct language exchange any such opposition is generally muted. When the king and the duke get him and Jim to address them by their supposed titles ('"Your Grace", or "My Lord," or "Your Lordship",' 164), Huck obliges. For he has already learnt from Pap 'that the best way to get along with his kind of people is to let them have their own way' (166).

The brilliance of Twain's novel however lies in the way that the powerful voices that sound within the novel's social world are contained by Huck's own narrating voice. Huck (and Jim's) voices are often, and finally, silenced in their social interaction, and their words have little or no effect. But it is Huck who, in terms of the novel's form, displays the various languages and value-systems of this south-western community and the ways in which they interact and relate to one another. And it is Huck's own voice in the narrative – for the telling of this narrative is the one thing he does control – that effectively (though usually unconsciously) challenges and tears the mask from all these surrounding languages. Thus, to take one very obvious example, Huck describes the Shephersons and Grangerfords in church with their guns 'between their knees or stood . . . handy against the wall' listening to some 'pretty ornery preaching – all about brotherly love, and such-like tiresomeness' (148). His laconic description reveals the sham that Christianity represents in a community ravaged by internecine violence and suggests how Southern concerns with codes of honour and proper (masculine) behaviour thinly disguise a horrific and brutal savagery. Huck recognises none of this explicitly, but Twain uses his narration to this end and to contest such values. Huck, then, is a relatively silent participant in many of the events described in the book, but the authority that his narrative gives him and the critical perspective it allows, perfectly balances and contests the varied (and more socially powerful) southern voices represented.

Huck ends the novel with silence and solitude before him, planning – in one of the most resonant closing lines in American literature – 'to light out for the Territory ahead of the rest' (366). Such a breaking-off of contact with his immediate world is a final measure of his social alienation. This can be seen as a hopeful ending, that paradigmatic American move to a new and unspoilt landscape where society might start over again. It is easier, though, to see it in more negative terms, for such pioneering commonly (as Huck's phrase suggests) paves the way for the reappearance of what one seeks to escape. And Huck's immediate future is to be potentially voiceless (with no one to talk to) and alone – and to be asocial is, by any larger human measure, scarcely to exist.

In focusing on Huck, I have temporarily put Jim's role in the novel to one side. I now return to that subject. I have suggested that Huck's narration provides a counter-balance to the voices and values of his surrounding social world. While this is true, we should not forget that he is also a product of this world, speaks its common language and shares many of its values. It is in the way that Twain uses Huck's narrative voice that its critical power lies. So, when Huck is wondering whether to write to Miss Watson to inform her that Jim is held as a runaway slave at the Phelpses, he 'give[s] up that notion' in part because 'she'd be mad and disgusted at his rascality and ungratefulness for leaving her, and so she'd sell him straight down the river again' (269). Huck's identity is necessarily constrained by the language and codes of his surrounding society and there is nothing here to suggest he is critical of Miss Watson's likely response. Twain, though, plays on the gap between the notion of Jim's 'rascality' and the reader's knowledge of what it means to be a slave, forced to serve a master or mistress against one's own free will, to release the irony that rings out so loudly. The text usually attains its other ironic and satiric effects in similar ways.

There is, however, something else in Huck's voice that cuts against any view of it as a device for the simple mouthing of surrounding racial and social prejudices. Shelley Fisher Fishkin, in her important book, *Was Huck Black?* (1993), suggests that Huck's voice may have been partly modelled on an African American source: that of the boy whose dialect is freely represented in Twain's short newspaper piece, 'Sociable Jimmy' (1874). She also shows Twain's debt to other African American cultural forms (such as 'signifying' and the trickster tale) in the writing of the novel. She consequently claims that the book, so celebrated for its representation of a distinctly 'American' vernacular style, has – both in its general content and in its particular syntax – African American roots; is a product of 'mixed literary bloodlines'.[41] I reduce Fishkin's argument here to the barest of essentials. The valuable connections she makes here, though, are part of a larger history of interchange between Euro-American and African American verbal and cultural forms that went on at a common and everyday level in the antebellum South (and has gone on ever since).

There is then, in *Huckleberry Finn*, a fluid racial politics at play. Huck may share elements of 'black' speech, but the words he often speaks are racist ones. When Jim first reveals his plan to go and work up North, to buy his wife out of slavery and his children too (or to have an Abolitionist steal them if their legal 'owner' refuses to sell), Huck is appalled. 'He wouldn't ever dared to talk such talk in his life before. . . . It was according to the old saying, "give a nigger an inch and he'll take an ell"' (124).

The novel's representation of race, then, and Huck's view of Jim, are complex. It is difficult to characterise Jim in the novel, as he is only ever seen through Huck's eyes and narrative. He shares Huck's outcast status in terms of social position and power, but is lower on such a scale than even this white-trash boy. Part of a relatively undifferentiated mass and called by a highly demeaning name ('By-and-by they fetched the niggers in and had prayers,' 20), his social value is as owned property, worth eight hundred dollars. His speech has no authority. He starts off the novel as he almost ends it, as the victim of Tom and Huck's practical jokes with no voice in whether or not Miss Watson sells him on (as she is thinking) down to New Orleans.

There has been much critical debate as to whether Jim is represented as a demeaning minstrel stereotype (the racist representation of the African American as uneducated, simple-minded, insensitive and unfailingly cheerful, common in all forms of popular entertainment in the period), or whether he is

s the passages describing Huck and Jim together on the raft that
nythic centre of the novel and which (we can assume) have appealed
eaders in so many different countries over the years. It is only here,
son's Island, that the voices of these two marginal figures are allowed
ely and (as far as we can tell) openly and in overall harmony with
r. This is not to deny that their agendas are different or that they may
y mislead each other at times. The raft is not a place without conflict.
trated by Jim's intransigence in arguments and by his own inability
vn his case, claims that 'you can't learn a nigger to argue' (114). Jim,
s plainly and shows anger toward Huck when he is tricked by him in
sing words which would be taboo in normal circumstances (calling
erson 'trash') and getting a genuine apology in response (121). The
is itself a fragile space, mown down by a steamboat, colonised by the
the duke, floating downriver ever deeper into slave territory.
of this, however, affects the utopian dimension to this relationship.
aft, the troubles and prejudices of river-bank life can largely (if provi-
) drop away. And the balance of the relationship, in the best moments,
ual one with both man and boy speaking when they will, with neither
ying to overwhelm or silence the other. The deep affection built up
n the two is sounded in the fondness of Jim's greeting to Huck imme-
following the feud ('I's mighty glad to git you back agin, honey,' 155),
Huck's musings in Chapter 31 on just how much Jim has cared for him,
n the pleasurable intimacy of the journey, 'a floating along, talking, and
g, and laughing' (271). The quality of Twain's prose captures the easy
anionship and the relaxed harmony of these scenes. It is Huck that speaks
we might construe things differently from Jim's perspective, but there is
rompt or necessity to do so.
either 'cramped up' nor 'smothery' like other places (156), on the raft the
can sit naked, their legs dangling in the water, enjoying the near-silences
u wouldn't hear nothing for you couldn't tell how long, except maybe frogs
omething' 159). Jim and Huck step outside the borders of the everyday
th-western community, alone together in nature, able to 'feel mighty free
d easy and comfortable' there (156). These passages are remarkable in both
eir lyrical power and their brevity. The image of Jim and Huck together on
e raft has become rooted in the American imagination, bringing black and
hite together in a dreamlike (yet very real – there are, for instance, 'dead
h laying around', 158) space, scarcely imaginable in actual social reality. The
hort sequences that describe and celebrate their union can be counted on the
ngers of one hand. This speaks, I would suggest, both to Twain's knowledge
f the intensity of the problems that have plagued relations between the races

presented as an intelligent and clear-thinking adult determinedly looking to
bring himself to as full a freedom as can be gained in the America of his time.
'Freedom' is indeed a key concept in this text. Huck's desire for freedom, to
escape constraining social bonds, is contrasted with Jim's wish to be free to *enter*
society, but up North, with the rights and responsibilities he has been previously denied. Seen from the outside, we can never quite know Jim or know
what motivates him. His words and actions may certainly be spurred in part
(as those of all slaves necessarily were) by the need to mask his real intentions
from his white listeners. On the raft he appears to speak openly and freely to
Huck, able to do so because of the latter's own low social status and boyhood
state. But even here we cannot be sure quite what is being masked and how far
he is using Huck to expedite his own plans. Does he, for instance, remain silent
about Pap's death to ensure that Huck still has a reason to continue down-river
with him: to protect his own best interests rather than Huck's feelings? Any
such speculation is bound to end in uncertainty. We can, however, see a clear
development in his representation as the novel progresses.

Jim starts the novel as owned property. Once he has escaped from slavery, we
see his fuller human and emotional dimensions, his hopes, and his future plans.
The descriptions of his words and actions in Huck's company allows David
L. Smith, for instance, to praise the novel for its 'explicitly anti-racist stand'
and to describe Jim himself as 'an intelligent, sensitive, wily, and considerate
individual', who in his person illustrates the fact that 'race provides no useful
index of character'.[42] But this fuller picture is quickly obliterated once the
king and the duke come on board the raft to direct operations. First Jim is
symbolically re-enslaved, to be tied 'hand and foot with a rope' (176) whenever
anyone else appears in view. Then, immediately following Jim's description
of the discovery of his daughter's deafness (which reveals the depth of his
family feelings and sensitivity), the king and the duke – who care little for his
feelings – fashion him into a grotesque 'outrage'. Painting his face 'a dead dull
solid blue', he 'didn't only look like he was dead, he looked considerable more
than that' (203–4). The metaphorical life is being drained out of Jim here.
His dehumanisation and devitalisation are then continued during the evasion
routine. The powerful independent voice that began to emerge with Huck on the
raft vanishes from sight. Jim becomes instead part of Tom Sawyer's game ('the
best fun [Tom] ever had in his life', 313) as he and Huck shape his imprisonment
and planned escape after the model of European romantic fiction, subjecting
him to acute physical discomfort and pain as they do so – filling his cabin
with rats and snakes and spiders, and hiding a piece of candlestick in his food,
'most mash[ing] all his teeth out' as a result (313). Jim's tormented black body
becomes here the source for Tom's (and to lesser extent, Huck's) entertainment.

As this happens, he necessarily slips back into stereotype, the unwilling but long-suffering butt of their extended comic routine.

This is the point of the narrative at which countless readers have criticised Twain for faulty planning and for inappropriate comic effect. In recent years, however, critics have suggested sound reasons for such apparently misguided plotting. This takes us back to the novel's historical background. Traditionally, the novel has been seen in the context of slavery. Jim's true and full humanity is accordingly revealed in his one-to-one relationship with Huck on the raft. While Huck's own innate moral goodness is shown in his decision to '*go to hell*' (272), rather than behaving as his southern social world would expect and revealing Jim's whereabouts to his owner. There is considerable power to this reading (despite the problem raised by terms like 'innate moral goodness' which seem to ignore issues of social conditioning completely). We are left here, though, with an obvious question. This echoes Aunt Sally's question to Tom, when she realises that Jim had in fact been given his freedom prior to the whole evasion episode, and that Tom knew this: 'what on earth did *you* want to set [Jim] free for, seeing he was already free?' (361). Why on earth, similarly, should Twain want to write an anti-slavery novel in the 1880s, long after the Civil War was over and more than twenty years after the African American, with Lincoln's Emancipation Proclamation of 1863, had officially been set 'free'? To ask this question is to suggest that the novel might be seen as entirely unchallenging, an exercise in conservative self-congratulation for its audience.

There is some problem in answering this. For Twain, dependent on his popularity for his living and with his reputation built on comic writing, usually tended to indirection and obliqueness when it came to challenging the dominant values and assumptions of his surrounding society (*The Gilded Age* is an exception). It is, accordingly, often difficult to work out his exact authorial intentions, a situation not helped by the fact that his own political and social attitudes were never entirely straightforward and coherent. It may be exactly this indeterminacy that has helped make his texts particularly adaptable to a variety of interpretations, and able to release new meanings according to the concerns and interests of each generation of critics who renegotiate them. Whatever the case, it is clear that as Twain's life continued, so his own awareness, and condemnation, of American racial injustices – and particularly the mistreatment of the African American community – greatly increased. Fishkin, indeed, in writing of Twain's 'insight into white racism toward blacks', claims that he 'subverted and challenged his culture's ingrained pieties with a boldness and subtlety that readers are still struggling to appreciate fully'.[43]

It is difficult, in *Huckleberry Finn*, t‹
one has recognised its subtlety, for it is
have convincingly interpreted the evas
politics of the post-Civil War years. Su
experience to see Twain as engaging – i
debate over race and civil rights occurrin‹
the United States to 'recognize and maint
slaves but this had not happened. African
of political and social liberation in the in
(the years 1866–77, when Congress reorga.
looked to find ways for white and African
in a 'free' society), but this did not last lon‹
'went free; stood a brief moment in the sun‹
slavery'.[44] For the white South (with the covert
of the nation as whole) gradually re-establishe
African American population, to enmesh the‹
web of oppression, whose interwoven econom‹
all reinforced one another'.[45] That web would re
down to the Civil Rights Movement of the 1960s

Jim's role, as portrayed in the evasion section
level) this larger historical reality. He has been free
been re-enslaved, and is kept in his prison-house
knowledge of that freedom. Jim suffers indignity an
from the two boys. Tom's supposed intention here
gained his own benefits from the situation) to rele
freedom. To present the episode in this way is to hi‹
as 'a satire on the way the United Sates botched the
slaves'.[46] Northerners increasingly lost interest in Africa
in their concern for sectional reconciliation after the
Codes' were introduced in southern states severely limi
slaves (and drastically restricting their voting rights). Sl
a share-cropping system, whereby white owners kept ult‹
land and continued to hold African Americans in financi
conditions went hand-in-hand with 'widespread vigilan‹
endemic racism'. 'The average freedman', 'in other words',
chance as Jim of realising any practical distinction between h
and his previous condition of servitude'.[47]

Jim's representation in this last sequence of the book (‹
reading it provokes) never, however, quite cancels out what w

read. For it
provide the
to so many
and on Jack
to speak fr‹
one anoth‹
deliberate‹
Huck, frus
to nail do‹
too, speak
the fog, u
a white p
raft, too,
king and
None
On the
sionally
is an e‹
voice t
betwe‹
diately
and i‹
and o
singi‹
comp
here:
no p
N
two
('y‹
or
so‹
an
th
th
w
fi
s
f

presented as an intelligent and clear-thinking adult determinedly looking to bring himself to as full a freedom as can be gained in the America of his time. 'Freedom' is indeed a key concept in this text. Huck's desire for freedom, to escape constraining social bonds, is contrasted with Jim's wish to be free to *enter* society, but up North, with the rights and responsibilities he has been previously denied. Seen from the outside, we can never quite know Jim or know what motivates him. His words and actions may certainly be spurred in part (as those of all slaves necessarily were) by the need to mask his real intentions from his white listeners. On the raft he appears to speak openly and freely to Huck, able to do so because of the latter's own low social status and boyhood state. But even here we cannot be sure quite what is being masked and how far he is using Huck to expedite his own plans. Does he, for instance, remain silent about Pap's death to ensure that Huck still has a reason to continue down-river with him: to protect his own best interests rather than Huck's feelings? Any such speculation is bound to end in uncertainty. We can, however, see a clear development in his representation as the novel progresses.

Jim starts the novel as owned property. Once he has escaped from slavery, we see his fuller human and emotional dimensions, his hopes, and his future plans. The descriptions of his words and actions in Huck's company allows David L. Smith, for instance, to praise the novel for its 'explicitly anti-racist stand' and to describe Jim himself as 'an intelligent, sensitive, wily, and considerate individual', who in his person illustrates the fact that 'race provides no useful index of character'.[42] But this fuller picture is quickly obliterated once the king and the duke come on board the raft to direct operations. First Jim is symbolically re-enslaved, to be tied 'hand and foot with a rope' (176) whenever anyone else appears in view. Then, immediately following Jim's description of the discovery of his daughter's deafness (which reveals the depth of his family feelings and sensitivity), the king and the duke – who care little for his feelings – fashion him into a grotesque 'outrage'. Painting his face 'a dead dull solid blue', he 'didn't only look like he was dead, he looked considerable more than that' (203–4). The metaphorical life is being drained out of Jim here. His dehumanisation and devitalisation are then continued during the evasion routine. The powerful independent voice that began to emerge with Huck on the raft vanishes from sight. Jim becomes instead part of Tom Sawyer's game ('the best fun [Tom] ever had in his life', 313) as he and Huck shape his imprisonment and planned escape after the model of European romantic fiction, subjecting him to acute physical discomfort and pain as they do so – filling his cabin with rats and snakes and spiders, and hiding a piece of candlestick in his food, 'most mash[ing] all his teeth out' as a result (313). Jim's tormented black body becomes here the source for Tom's (and to lesser extent, Huck's) entertainment.

As this happens, he necessarily slips back into stereotype, the unwilling but long-suffering butt of their extended comic routine.

This is the point of the narrative at which countless readers have criticised Twain for faulty planning and for inappropriate comic effect. In recent years, however, critics have suggested sound reasons for such apparently misguided plotting. This takes us back to the novel's historical background. Traditionally, the novel has been seen in the context of slavery. Jim's true and full humanity is accordingly revealed in his one-to-one relationship with Huck on the raft. While Huck's own innate moral goodness is shown in his decision to '*go* to hell' (272), rather than behaving as his southern social world would expect and revealing Jim's whereabouts to his owner. There is considerable power to this reading (despite the problem raised by terms like 'innate moral goodness' which seem to ignore issues of social conditioning completely). We are left here, though, with an obvious question. This echoes Aunt Sally's question to Tom, when she realises that Jim had in fact been given his freedom prior to the whole evasion episode, and that Tom knew this: 'what on earth did *you* want to set [Jim] free for, seeing he was already free?' (361). Why on earth, similarly, should Twain want to write an anti-slavery novel in the 1880s, long after the Civil War was over and more than twenty years after the African American, with Lincoln's Emancipation Proclamation of 1863, had officially been set 'free'? To ask this question is to suggest that the novel might be seen as entirely unchallenging, an exercise in conservative self-congratulation for its audience.

There is some problem in answering this. For Twain, dependent on his popularity for his living and with his reputation built on comic writing, usually tended to indirection and obliqueness when it came to challenging the dominant values and assumptions of his surrounding society (*The Gilded Age* is an exception). It is, accordingly, often difficult to work out his exact authorial intentions, a situation not helped by the fact that his own political and social attitudes were never entirely straightforward and coherent. It may be exactly this indeterminacy that has helped make his texts particularly adaptable to a variety of interpretations, and able to release new meanings according to the concerns and interests of each generation of critics who renegotiate them. Whatever the case, it is clear that as Twain's life continued, so his own awareness, and condemnation, of American racial injustices – and particularly the mistreatment of the African American community – greatly increased. Fishkin, indeed, in writing of Twain's 'insight into white racism toward blacks', claims that he 'subverted and challenged his culture's ingrained pieties with a boldness and subtlety that readers are still struggling to appreciate fully'.[43]

It is difficult, in *Huckleberry Finn*, to see the boldness of this challenge, until one has recognised its subtlety, for it is far from self-evident. But recent critics have convincingly interpreted the evasion sequence in the light of the racial politics of the post-Civil War years. Such readings look at African American experience to see Twain as engaging – in an allegorical way – in the ongoing debate over race and civil rights occurring at that time. Lincoln had committed the United States to 'recognize and maintain the freedom' of the emancipated slaves but this had not happened. African Americans had gained some degree of political and social liberation in the immediate period of Reconstruction (the years 1866–77, when Congress reorganised the South after the War, and looked to find ways for white and African American to live equally together in a 'free' society), but this did not last long. 'The slave', in DuBois's words, 'went free; stood a brief moment in the sun; then moved back again toward slavery'.[44] For the white South (with the covert – and sometimes overt – support of the nation as whole) gradually re-established authority and control over its African American population, to enmesh them all over again 'in a seamless web of oppression, whose interwoven economic, political, and social strands all reinforced one another'.[45] That web would remain more or less intact right down to the Civil Rights Movement of the 1960s.

Jim's role, as portrayed in the evasion section, mirrors (at an individual level) this larger historical reality. He has been freed by his owner but has since been re-enslaved, and is kept in his prison-house by Tom, despite the boy's knowledge of that freedom. Jim suffers indignity and various painful torments from the two boys. Tom's supposed intention here is eventually (once he has gained his own benefits from the situation) to release him once more into freedom. To present the episode in this way is to historicise it and to read it as 'a satire on the way the United Sates botched the enterprise of freeing its slaves'.[46] Northerners increasingly lost interest in African American civil rights in their concern for sectional reconciliation after the War. A series of 'Black Codes' were introduced in southern states severely limiting the rights of freed slaves (and drastically restricting their voting rights). Slavery was replaced by a share-cropping system, whereby white owners kept ultimate control of their land and continued to hold African Americans in financial dependency. Such conditions went hand-in-hand with 'widespread vigilante intimidation and endemic racism'. 'The average freedman', 'in other words', 'had about as much chance as Jim of realising any practical distinction between his current situation and his previous condition of servitude'.[47]

Jim's representation in this last sequence of the book (and the historical reading it provokes) never, however, quite cancels out what we have previously read. For it is the passages describing Huck and Jim together on the raft that provide the mythic centre of the novel and which (we can assume) have appealed to so many readers in so many different countries over the years. It is only here, and on Jackson's Island, that the voices of these two marginal figures are allowed to speak freely and (as far as we can tell) openly and in overall harmony with one another. This is not to deny that their agendas are different or that they may deliberately mislead each other at times. The raft is not a place without conflict. Huck, frustrated by Jim's intransigence in arguments and by his own inability to nail down his case, claims that 'you can't learn a nigger to argue' (114). Jim, too, speaks plainly and shows anger toward Huck when he is tricked by him in the fog, using words which would be taboo in normal circumstances (calling a white person 'trash') and getting a genuine apology in response (121). The raft, too, is itself a fragile space, mown down by a steamboat, colonised by the king and the duke, floating downriver ever deeper into slave territory.

None of this, however, affects the utopian dimension to this relationship. On the raft, the troubles and prejudices of river-bank life can largely (if provisionally) drop away. And the balance of the relationship, in the best moments, is an equal one with both man and boy speaking when they will, with neither voice trying to overwhelm or silence the other. The deep affection built up between the two is sounded in the fondness of Jim's greeting to Huck immediately following the feud ('I's mighty glad to git you back agin, honey,' 155), and in Huck's musings in Chapter 31 on just how much Jim has cared for him, and on the pleasurable intimacy of the journey, 'a floating along, talking, and singing, and laughing' (271). The quality of Twain's prose captures the easy companionship and the relaxed harmony of these scenes. It is Huck that speaks here: we might construe things differently from Jim's perspective, but there is no prompt or necessity to do so.

Neither 'cramped up' nor 'smothery' like other places (156), on the raft the two can sit naked, their legs dangling in the water, enjoying the near-silences ('you wouldn't hear nothing for you couldn't tell how long, except maybe frogs or something' 159). Jim and Huck step outside the borders of the everyday south-western community, alone together in nature, able to 'feel mighty free and easy and comfortable' there (156). These passages are remarkable in both their lyrical power and their brevity. The image of Jim and Huck together on the raft has become rooted in the American imagination, bringing black and white together in a dreamlike (yet very real – there are, for instance, 'dead fish laying around', 158) space, scarcely imaginable in actual social reality. The short sequences that describe and celebrate their union can be counted on the fingers of one hand. This speaks, I would suggest, both to Twain's knowledge of the intensity of the problems that have plagued relations between the races in America and to the deep-seated nature of the desire to overcome them. This is, to stress once more, Huck's view of his and Jim's relationship. But that does not alter the fact that this projection of generous interracial ease and harmony offered a model of equality, empathy and social possibility, even in a historical time of intractable racial difference and friction, when any practical resolution to such problems had vanished from sight. That is the ultimate power of Twain's great book.

A Connecticut Yankee and *Pudd'nhead Wilson*

Twain has the reputation as the most American of authors but he was also, as I suggest earlier, one of the most cosmopolitan. He was highly aware of the way that American culture both depended on – and differed from – the Old World. In *Huckleberry Finn*, he has 'the duke' garble the ennobled Shakespearian word to carnival effect: 'But soft you, the fair Ophelia:/Ope not thy ponderous and marble jaws,/But get thee to a nunnery – go!' (179). And he undermines official literary hierarchies in giving full voice to a common American vernacular, with all its qualities – homely, incisive, comic, sentimental and poetic, by turn. But elsewhere, and often, he sets his fictions in Europe, with European protagonists.

Indeed, *The Prince and the Pauper* (1881), set in England and taking English history as its subject, remains one of his best known books, as well as being his only novel that was, from the first, written for children. The frontispiece to the novel consists of a letter from Hugh Latimer (Bishop of Worcester) to Lord Cromwell on the birth of the future Edward VI. It is written in the standard style of Latimer's day – a style which makes the reading of *Huckleberry Finn*'s non-standard nineteenth-century American English easy as pie in comparison ('Gode gyffe us alle grace, to yelde dew thankes to our Lorde Gode, Gode of Inglonde, for verely He hathe shoyd Hym selff Gode of Inglonde . . .'). Twain follows this with 'The quality of mercy' quote from the *Merchant of Venice*, but here with no comic garbling introduced. Within the main body of the novel, the author immerses himself in the history of the short reign of Henry VIII's only male Tudor heir (his son by Jane Seymour), focusing in part on the cruelties and violence of the times.

But Twain's main plot device and the questions that it raises are familiar ones. The novel turns on the twinned relationship between the prince, Edward and the pauper, Tom Canty and the problems over identity – and indeed how we might define that term – raised by their exchange of roles. Divisive class difference and aristocratic privilege, the distinguishing marks of a British feudal as opposed to an American democratic culture, both feature strongly in the book, while Tom's successful role-play suggests the complete artificiality of such hierarchies. The very nature of the novel as children's fiction, however, prevents the deeper exploration of such concerns.

In 1896, Twain would publish another historical novel set entirely in Europe, the book that he sometimes saw as his all-time best work: *Personal Recollections of Joan of Arc.* The reasons for this massive failure of judgement are easy to pinpoint. They include his attraction toward what has since become known as the cult of true womanhood (the belief that ideal womanliness consists in a submissive domesticity and the virtues of purity and piety). For 'despite her air of authority and proficiency on the battle-field, Twain's Joan is a domestic angel. . . . [W]illingly subject to male authority of all kinds . . . her self-sacrifice makes her the truest of True Women'.[48] They are explained, too, both by his own liking for historical fiction as a genre and in the fact that Joan herself was so clearly modelled on his daughter Susie, who died so unexpectedly (and with a devastating effect on Twain and his family) in the same year as the novel's publication.

From the early years of his celebrity, Twain had been fascinated by British history and culture and how they might be used to measure, and reflect on, American values and their strengths and weaknesses. In England, in 1872, he would write a preface for an English edition of *Innocents Abroad*, commenting that 'Our kindred blood & our common language, our kindred religion & political liberty, make us feel nearer to England than to other nations' (*L5*, 120). This was followed more privately in his journal by his saying: 'I do like these English people – they are perfectly splendid – & so says every American who has staid here any length of time' (*L5*, 628). By the point in the later 1880s when he wrote *A Connecticut Yankee in King Arthur's Court* (1889) his attitude had changed.[49] His more critical approach to British culture was largely in response to Matthew Arnold and the transatlantic dialogue stimulated by essays such as his 'A Word About America' (1882) and the more famous 'Civilisation in the United States' (April, 1888). For Arnold, touching on a topic particularly close to Twain's heart, criticised the 'craving for amusement' that had produced the enthusiasm for comic writing in America. More fundamentally, he judged 'industrialism' and 'culture' to be contradictory concepts and implied that America was a place of vulgar manners, 'limited in its culture, and . . . unconscious of its limitation'. America, he charged, was a philistine country, too greatly dependent on material comforts and conveniences: 'A great void exists in the civilisation over there'.[50]

Twain may have misunderstood the crux of Arnold's points – for Arnold was not so much arguing Britain's superiority over America, but rather the failings of any civilisation built on materialist values. But he was swift to respond to the slurs that he saw, dismissing the British writer's much-vaunted civilisation as superficial, 'worm-eaten' and only suitable for 'slave-making ants'. 'Any system which had in it . . . human slavery, despotic government, inequality, . . . brutal punishments for crimes, superstition almost universal, and dirt and poverty almost universal' was judged 'not a real civilisation'. While America's ability to measure up to such a definition was proved by the fact that most of its citizens possessed 'liberty, equality, plenty to eat . . . abundance of churches, newspapers, libraries . . . and a good education'.[51]

A Connecticut Yankee in King Arthur's Court

This debate with Arnold clearly sets the early terms for *Connecticut Yankee*. Hank Morgan's fantastic transfer from the Colt Arms factory in nineteenth-century Hartford to Camelot and sixth-century Arthurian England provides an allegorical device to explore the British-American cultural divide. Thus, on the American side, we have Hank Morgan, a pragmatic mechanic and representative of a developing industrial culture. Hank's inventive skills have taken him beyond his father's trade as a blacksmith, to become 'head superintendent' at 'the great arms factory' – the Colts Firearms Manufactory – in Hartford, Connecticut (20). His tastes are unsophicated. In his Hartford home 'you couldn't go into a room but you would find an insurance-chromo, or at least a three-color God-Bless-Our-Home over the door; and in the parlor we had nine' (84). But if he is a philistine, he is unconscious of his own cultural limitations. Comfort is more important to him than high culture – he immediately notices the lack of gas-lighting, window-glass, carpets, sugar, coffee and tobacco in Camelot, all 'the little conveniences that make the real comfort of life' (83–5).

Knocked out by a crowbar by one of his factory underlings, Hank regains consciousness to find himself transported to sixth-century England. Noting plentiful opportunities for 'a man of knowledge, brains, pluck and enterprise' (96), he determines to 'boss the whole country inside of three months' (36). This is precisely what he then does. The metaphor he uses for this opportunity – 'I couldn't keep from thinking about it . . . just as one does who has struck oil' (96) – firmly positions him as part of a go-getting American modernity, one who will quickly convert the natural (and human) resources around him to his own profit.

But if Hank represents vulgar materialism and Gilded Age opportunistic enterprise, Twain uses him to make the 'worm-eaten' state of British culture clear. That the novel speaks of the nineteenth-century present as well as the Arthurian past is indicated in his authorial prefacing remark:

> It is not pretended that . . . the ungentle laws and customs touched upon in this tale . . . existed in England in the sixth century; no, it is only pretended that inasmuch as they existed in the English and other civilizations of far later times, it is safe to consider that it is no libel upon the sixth century to suppose them to have been in practice in that day also. (xv)

The use of the word 'civilization' here suggests Twain may well have Arnold (and his 'Civilisation in the United States') directly in mind as he writes.

To read *Connecticut Yankee* is almost to imagine Twain ticking off the boxes that indicate Arthurian England's lack of civilised values. 'Human slavery' is the basis on which this entire society rests:

> The most of King Arthur's British nation were slaves, pure and simple, and bore that name, and wore the iron collar on their necks; and the rest were slaves in fact, but without the name. . . . The truth was, the nation as a body was in the world for one object . . . only: to grovel before king and Church and noble; to slave for them, sweat blood for them, . . . work that they might play, . . . be familiar all their lives with degrading language and postures of adulation that they might walk in pride. . . .   (98)

All but the opening part of Hank's words here readily translate to the Britain of Twain's own times, a society with institutional structures still based on the monarchy, an inherited nobility and an established church.

Arthur's England has become, under the power of the Catholic Church, a 'nation of worms' (100). The despotic Church works hand in glove with an autocratic form of government to rule over this superstitious people. Hank is initially 'mere dirt' to the Arthurians because of his lack of 'pedigree' or title' (100), but it is the literal 'dirt and poverty' that he first notices, and that characterises the kingdom at large. He sees men 'with long, coarse, uncombed hair that hung down over their faces and made them look like animals', and town streets composed of 'muck and swine, and naked brats . . . and shabby huts' (28–9). The family suffering from smallpox, visited by Hank and King Arthur later in the novel, have had everything of value stripped by Church and feudal lord: 'everything had a ruined look, and [was] eloquent of poverty' (369). Soap is generally noticeable by its absence (83), something Hank looks to remedy as, in the manner of other late nineteenth-century colonialists, he brings that article, along with his civilisation, to this backward land.

America, in contrast, is associated with freedom and good and democratic government. From the first, Hank bases his operations on his dislike of the autocracy and his alternative set of political principles. When he congratulates his army, at the end of the narrative, on annihilating the enemy that would roll back all his various reforms, he addresses the soldiers as 'champions of human liberty and equality', words that he capitalises (556). His earlier proclamation of a Republic, soon after hearing of Arthur's death, is based on American democratic principle:

> all political power has reverted to its original source, the people of the nation . . . ; wherefore there is no longer a nobility, no longer a privileged class, no longer an Established Church: all men are become exactly equal, they are upon one common level, and religion is free.   (544)

And, in Chapter 9, Hank's speaks of his dedication to a free press. He indicates his intention, 'by and by . . . to start a newspaper. The first thing you want in a new country, is a patent office; then work up your school system; and after that, out with your paper' (109). Schools and newspapers are, accordingly, soon in place.

We make the connection between the England Hank visits and that of Arnold's own time, mainly through the ongoing existence of a monarchy, aristocracy and powerful Established Church. Such links are reinforced in other ways: by the use in the illustrations, for example, of Tennyson as the model for Merlin. Looked at in this way, a straightforward set of oppositions seem to emerge between England and America, feudalism and democracy, slavery and freedom, ignorance and education, science and superstition, the past and the present, and so on. But whenever such oppositions are used as a tool by which to approach Twain's novels (and this tactic is always useful in starting to explore the meanings of any text), we find apparently firm contrasts dissolving and something more complex taking their place. This novel proves no exception to that rule.

So, in *Connecticut Yankee*, Hank puts himself forward as the voice of democratic equality, but he is also quick to separate himself off from those who surround him: 'Here I was, a giant among pygmies, . . . a master intelligence among intellectual moles' (102). The title he assumes, 'The Boss', is given him by one of the mass of the nation, a blacksmith and Hank values it accordingly (102–3). But that title in fact merely reflects the more-or-less absolute power that he seeks and quickly gets. He is appointed Arthur's executive minister as a result of trickery: apparently in command of nature's phenomena, he has in fact realised an eclipse of the sun is to occur and times his prediction of it accordingly. He thus becomes 'the second personage in the Kingdom, as far as political power and authority were concerned. . . . I was no shadow of a king; I was the substance. . . . My power was colossal' (83, 96). Both his title and his actions while holding that position (whatever his final democratic intent) make him as autocratic as those he would replace.

This is confirmed in a particularly revealing manner when Hank visits the castle of the wicked Morgan le Fay. The match of names (Morgan) alerts the reader to the similarity that, to some degree, undermines their differences. Her casual stabbing of her handsome page-boy, slipping 'a dirk into him in as matter-of-course a way as another person would have harpooned a rat' (196), is in accord with her royal prerogative. Hank, accordingly, judges her lack of compassion or remorse to be a result of training, rather than of moral culpability. (The implications of this judgement are crucial to the developing determinist strain in Twain's thought and his increasingly strong challenge to the notions of individual moral agency and distinct and autonomous selfhood. In this respect, Twain's voice seems to merge with Hank. For if 'training is all there is *to* a person', with all her or his thoughts and opinions 'merely heredity and training', then 'all that is original in us' disappears more or less completely from view, 'can be covered up and hidden by the point of a cambric needle', 217.) In this same series of episodes, however, the queen orders the composer of the song played at the royal banquet by a badly-rehearsed band to be hanged. Consequently awed by Hank's supposed occult powers, she consults him on the matter. Not wanting to be unreasonable, Hank 'considered the matter thoughtfully, and ended by having the musicians . . . play that Sweet Bye and Bye [the song in question] again, which they did. Then I saw that she was right, and gave her permission to hang the whole band' (206).

It would be wrong to make too much of this incident, as it is clear that Twain just took the opportunity for a good joke. It does nonetheless indicate the more callous side of Hank. A showman in the Tom Sawyer mode, but in adult form, he generally holds his various audiences in some contempt. He describes 'a thousand acres of human beings groveling on the ground' (91) when he uses blasting-powder to blow up Merlin's tower – a feat he puts down to his own greater power as a magician. Indeed, the performances he puts on and the effects he creates, come recurrently to outweigh the humanitarian qualities he also possesses. When he and the King travel the kingdom in peasant-dress disguise, Hank deals with the threat of charging knights by throwing a dynamite bomb and apparently delights in the resulting 'steady drizzle of microscopic fragments of knights and hardware and horse-flesh' (355). Later, he personally takes on the challenge of the destruction of Arthurian knight-errantry, 'entering the lists [as] . . . the champion of hard unsentimental common-sense and reason' (498) and dressed apparently to kill – though with laughter rather than violence – in 'flesh-colored tights from neck to heel' and 'blue silk puffings about my loins' (499). Such humour, though and the early comic spectacle of Hank lassooing the clumsy and armour-bound charging knights from their horses, then disappear as he 'bag[s]' nine of an oncoming five hundred knights with his 'dragoon revolver' to halt their charge (506–7).

This takes us back to Hank's initial description of his work at Colt's, and his ability to make 'guns, revolvers, cannon . . . all sorts of labor-saving machinery' (20). Hank's rationalism and modernity has a steely and destructive edge to it. The further the book proceeds, the more he seems a natural-born killer whose actions come to rival and outdo Morgan le Fay's culturally-sanctioned violence. His role as the technocrat hero who fosters and celebrates American democratic values fades as, instead, he becomes the agent of colonialist rule who imposes his authority and value-system on the mass of the population by increasingly brutal means. As this occurs, his technological abilities become cause for abhorrence rather than admiration, especially in the concluding Battle of the Sand-Belt scenes. Faced by a rebellion instigated by the Church, Hank prepares to dynamite the 'vast factories, mills, workshops, magazines, etc.' (541) composing his new England. He holes up with his remaining supporters, fifty-two young boys who have been under Hank's 'training from seven to ten years' (540), and who are consequently – and unlike the other 'human muck' in the kingdom (551) – still loyal to his values.

He then defends his camp by means of gatling guns, dynamite torpedoes, a series of electric fences and a water-filled ditch, and destroys the twenty-five thousand armed men who face him through that weaponry. Hank's cave contains a 'big dynamo' (541) which powers the electric wires and also lights up the scenes of slaughter he releases: 'I touched a button and set fifty electric suns aflame' (564). His scientific knowledge, presented here as god-like in its power, is thus finally shown to have dystopian rather than utopian implications. The man who would be boss and light-bringer at one and the same time ends up instead as a mass murderer. It may be no coincidence then that in an earlier sequence, when Hank uses germanic incantations to accompany his supposed 'magic', a part of one of the words he chants is 'massenmenchen-moerder' (292).

Any differences between Arthurian and late nineteenth-century values and the different forms of government and social systems in the two periods, are largely forgotten in the slaughter loosed by Hank's technology at the book's end. The Victorian era is generally associated with a sense of evolutionary optimism (as expressed in the work of the social philosopher Herbert Spencer). According to such thinking, scientific, social and political advances were gradually and inevitably improving the human condition. The First World War was the cataclysm that would finally blow such a progressive vision sky-high. The ending of *Connecticut Yankee* now reads as prescient in its foreshadowing of this later historical event and its larger philosophical impact. Twain's novel is cyclic. It opens in the dark ages and eventually ends there, with all evidence of Hank's reforms finally wiped out. Any idea of historical evolution is exploded and replaced by reversion – the move back to an original state of savagery, Arthur's world as it was before Hank came. In his later *Secret History of Eddypus*, Twain would again depict history as a dark cycle, marked by 'a human tendency toward dictatorship on the one hand and subservience and fanaticism on the other'.[52]

The differences between Hank's social engineering and Arthurian feudal practice also blurs in other ways as the novel progresses. One of Hank's prime aims is to abolish slavery in the country and Arthur – after discovering the real meaning of slavery while travelling the country in disguise alongside Hank – finally takes on Lincoln's role as emancipator. (It is indeed possible to interpret the novel as an allegory of ante bellum North-South relationships in the US). Hank's new civilisation, however, one which mirrors the time and country from which he comes, is not without its own forms of 'slavery'. For his 'new deal' (160) – the improved society he aims to introduce – needs suitable men to run it. Hank sends such candidates he runs across to his 'Man-Factory' (160) for this purpose: 'a Factory where I'm going to turn groping and grubbing automata into *men*' (212). 'Automata', with its direct association with the mechanical, forms an appropriate link with Hank's use of the word 'factory', and both words together suggest the dehumanising (rather than the humanising) aspects of his project. Moreover, such forms of discourse remind us that Twain is writing his book at 'a critical cultural moment [in American history] in which relations between the labour, bodies, and agency, were being (re) invented, renegotiated'.[53]

For the increasing mechanisation of labour, an expanding factory system and a rapidly growing economy were radically altering the relations between labour and capital in America at the time. As this happened, so a certain crisis in masculinity occurred. For the male worker was becoming little more than a cog in the larger industrial machine, with the independence he believed he possessed in danger of erasure. Hank's unfeeling manipulations of the human material at his disposal mirrors such late nineteenth-century realities (see my commentary earlier on the hermit and the making of shirts in the valley of Holiness). He accordingly stands as the representative of a new social and economic regime where workers are treated as mere fodder in the search for increased profit. And when we turn our attention back from the production of material goods to the training of men we see similar dehumanising implications in his actions. The fifty-two boys follow his orders in the Sand-Belt massacre because they have been trained within his system rather than having had (like the rest of the nation) their initial teaching from the church. The question this raises is whether they, then, have any more free will and agency than the fellow-citizens they oppose? And if Hank does abolish slavery as an institution in the land, is that bowing hermit and each of those boys anything more than a different type of slave?

My approach to this novel is selective and more emphasis is needed on its humorous aspects: the way Twain reworks history and legend, burlesques Malory's *Morte D'Arthur* and sets modern and medieval practices and belief-systems in comic juxtaposition. More attention, too, might be given to the picaresque form of the book and the sheer variety of the incident it contains. My emphasis, rather, has been on the way the oppositions that structure the book collapse in on one another.[54] Many of these contrasts seem first set up to aid Twain in his defence of modern American civilisation in the light of Arnold's critique. Thus that defence, too, is drastically undermined.

A similar collapse can also be identified in the main character conflict in the book – between Hank Morgan and Merlin, (for Hank) the very representative of Arthurian ignorance and superstition. For the sharp lines between Hank's science and Merlin's magic increasingly blur as the narrative proceeds. Hank's reputation in Arthur's England, gained from his knowledge and manipulation of science and technology, is that of a 'mighty magician' (86). His book-long contest with Merlin takes the form of a series of encounters: among them, the blowing up of Merlin's tower, the restoration of the well in the valley of Holiness and the duel over the future of knight-errantry. Hank's 'miracles' may be science-based but his visible methods (the use of dramatic effect and incantation) are indistinguishable from his rival. Throughout the novel, Merlin's supposed magic is apparently subject to inevitable defeat by Hank's modern and marvellous skills. But in a complete reverse, at its end, Merlin uses his magic to send Hank into a thirteen-century sleep, before he himself lands up against the electric wires and dies, 'a petrified laugh' of triumph still on his face (570). The fact that Merlin literally has the last laugh, however necessary this may be for the novel's plot, jolts the reader's expectations and upsets the firm sense of difference in power and ability constructed between the two figures.

Hank, then, in the tactics he uses and in the descriptions of the way he works his effects, 'keeps turning *into* Merlin'.[55] So, as the novel proceeds, he also becomes more and more closely a part of the Arthurian world he initially scorns. His final defence, against the might of the nation, of the regime that he has established, sees him inhabiting Merlin's cave. By the end of the novel's action, he is speaking in Arthurian phrases such as 'Wit ye well' (18), and is literally wedded to its world, married to Sandy. Finally, he is alien to the modern universe to which he returns, left 'a stranger and forlorn' (574) as he grieves for his lost family and his 'lost land' (26).

By this point, a radical destabilisation has occurred. Hank's late nineteenth-century American value-system has proved, in many ways, as flawed as the one it would replace. And it is Arthur, previously scorned as the representative of monarchical privilege (97–8), who provides the book's one genuine moment of heroism, carrying a dying girl to her mother in the smallpox hut. The progressive model of history Hank shares with his fellow-Victorians has been exposed as illusory in the extreme violence of the novel's ending. This has caused him (in the novel's postscript) to retreat to a dream of comforting domesticity. Such a movement – the rejection of public history in favour of the private and domestic life – would become the norm for a later generation of modernist writers, Virginia Woolf and Hemingway among them. Indeed, one critic convincingly argues that in this book Twain 'signs himself in modernity's sunderings'.[56]

Certainly this text – like so many other Twain novels too – moves in contradictory directions, with no easy closure to the various problems it addresses. Twain tended to look at the world through a series of different lenses. His own comparative viewpoint was echoed in his larger recognition of how partial-sighted all human beings are, constrained by their various limits, prejudices, and value systems. He gives an allegorical illustration of such limits in *Connecticut Yankee* when Hank describes the prisoner in Morgan le Fay's dungeon. Over the years, this man has witnessed the funerals of his family-members through a crack the width of an arrow-slit in his cell wall. It turns out that these are fraudulent, staged by the queen 'to scorch his heart with' (225). This brief incident cuts right to the heart of Twain's larger fictional enterprise. The prisoner's vision is partial and necessarily inaccurate. So Twain constantly sets one straitjacketed way of seeing against another and explores the complexities and problems that result when they are juxtaposed. At the same time, he never loses sight of multiplicity – of the many ways of seeing that compose our world and of the advantages of being aware of, and understanding, as many of them as possible.

My analysis of *A Connecticut Yankee* starts with Twain's response to Matthew Arnold, but shows how any attempt to restrict our reading of the novel to a celebration of American 'civilisation' soon runs into difficulty. Similarly, any attempt to construct an exact allegorical fit between sixth-century England and its Victorian equivalent can only work to a partial extent. We can read Twain's book, too, through an American, as well as a transnational, lens – as an allegorical exploration of late-nineteenth-century class relationships, regional identities, and/or white-indian disputes (the Arthurians are indeed called 'white Indians', 40). This is not to downplay Twain's dispute with Arnold or to marginalise its importance in his writing of the book. But it does seem that as he worked out that dispute in literary terms, Twain found himself losing confidence in his own culture and any sense of its superiority. In the 1892 *The American Claimant* – a patchy but interesting and under-noticed book – Twain would continue his dispute with Arnold. This time, though, and despite his continued praise of the American press – see Mr Parker's speech to the Mechanics' Club (98–9) – he explicitly criticises the hypocrisies and failures of America's own supposedly democratic and egalitarian society.

Hank Morgan starts the book as a potential technocratic and democratic hero. As it progresses, however, he becomes too often more concerned with his own dramatic performances than with the welfare of the Arthurian people he would help. More, the representation of Hank's attempts as civilised light-bringer to impose the value system of his own society on that of a primitive 'other' clearly prefigures Twain's later explicit attacks on turn-of-the-century Western imperialism and its results. It is easy to see Hank here as ugly American,[57] so confident of his American value scheme that he will impose it single-mindedly and rapidly on others with no sense of its inappropriateness to their circumstances, and with no idea of the inevitable violent reaction it will cause. Twain here, at an early historical stage, envisions a whole series of later and very real American expeditions abroad.

Twain and genre

As I move from *Connecticut Yankee* to *Pudd'nhead Wilson*, I return briefly to Twain's use of realism, and his departures from it. This follows the previous discussion of this subject. It is noticeable that none of Twain's four best-known novels (examined in this chapter) is set in his own historical period or offers any direct representation of contemporary America and its social problems. And, in my view, of these four, only *Huckleberry Finn* can be properly considered as a realist text. *A Connecticut Yankee* is a fantasy, while *Pudd'nhead Wilson* – if it is considered with its twin text, *Those Extraordinary Twins* – veers from farce to tragedy. And with its flattened characters, strongly determining circumstances and stress on plot rather than expansive description, it seems as close to allegory as to any other mode.

Twain's fiction undoubtedly did explore the historical circumstances of late nineteenth-century American life. It addresses such varied issues as race and reconstruction, modernisation and its effects, class difference, boyhood and masculinity and the relationship between the two, capitalism and an enterprise culture, personal agency, the law, etc. But he usually approached such topics in a highly indirect way. Their seriousness and contemporary relevance are generally thickly disguised by the genres and settings he uses and by his comic forms. Ultimately, his celebrity and his success relied on his humor, not on his increasingly bleak view of human nature and of American life at the century's end – and Twain knew this only too well.

Twain, then, conveyed his judgements on the American world around him through the play of a number of literary forms. And only by *retreating* from any transparent representation of immediate reality could he do so. Most writers whom we would now group under a 'realist' label saw it, rather, as their task to observe and exactly describe the new and rapidly changing features of late nineteenth-century society. Alongside other 'experts' – sociologists, city planners and the like – they looked to map the contours of this society 'with assiduous care both to material and to ideological detail'.[58] Such mapping went alongside the extended representation of the life-style, personal interactions and thoughts and feelings of the protagonists who negotiated this larger social world. This was not Twain's way. Indeed, he acknowledged his own difficulties with such close observation of interpersonal relationships when he wrote to Howells in late 1899: 'Ah, if I could look into the insides of people as you do, & put it on paper, & invent things for them to do & say, & tell *how* they said it, I could write a fine & readable book . . .' (*THL*, 710).

Howells was the foremost 'realist' of his day. His fiction has a strongly developed sense of city location (both interiors and exteriors), and of the way his protagonists inhabit them. His detailed descriptions of place and of character – and of the latter's motivations and conversations – together build the 'solidity of specification' which glues his novels together. Twain relies, instead, on picaresque forms, movements through a variety of locations and on action, and sometimes adventure, rather than on introspection. Individual scene and incident, and frequent and climactic action, often at the fringes of the settled social world, tend to replace an extended focus on scene and character, and their gradual and detailed development.

Pudd'nhead Wilson

In *Pudd'nhead Wilson* (1894), Twain returns to the Mississippi Valley setting of *Tom Sawyer* and *Huckleberry Finn* to write a much bleaker novel, and the last major fiction published in his lifetime. Twain does introduce setting with some care and detail at the start of this book, describing the 'snug little collection of modest one- and two-story [white-washed] frame dwellings' that compose the town of Dawson's Landing, and its main street with its occasional brick store, 'three stories high tower[ing] above interjected bunches of little frame shops'. But the impression of studied domesticity conveyed (as he depicts the rose-vines, pots of geraniums, and even the sleeping cat typical of these 'pretty homes') is silently contrasted with Dawson's Landing's status as 'a slave-holding town'.

'[S]leepy, and comfortable and contented' (17–20), everything about the town's appearance belies the harsher reality that slavery speaks. For there is no comfortable lazing around for the owned human property who live here. We remember the analogy between a slave and a dog in *Tom Sawyer* as we are now told of Percy Driscoll, that he was 'a fairly humane man toward slaves and other animals' (35). And there is little contentment, or real sense of 'home', for those who (or whose children) may be sold down river and away from house and family on the master's slightest whim. The reference, too, to shops (and shopping) serves to measure the daily business of white family and community life against the status of the town's slaves: both trading commodities and the unpaid labour helping to produce the community's wealth. The opening of this novel, in other words, depends not on the full transparency that generally marks the realist text but on *irony*, the gap between what things appear to be and their underlying reality.

That irony is then deepened with the introduction of Roxy and what we learn about her. Roxana, Twain's only major African American female character, is first introduced by way of her voice, overheard in shouted conversation with Jasper by the book's title character, David Wilson, as he works on his accounts. The third-person narrator reports the 'idle and aimless jabber' of these two slaves. So Jasper's words, 'I's gwine to come a-court'n' yo bimeby, Roxy', are answered by her: '*You* is, you black mud-cat! Yah – yah – yah! I got somep'n' better to do den 'sociat'n' wid niggers as black as you is. Is ole Miss Cooper's Nancy done give you de mitten?' (30–31). The move in a few pages from the white-washed exteriors of the town to the blackness of an African American's skin, and from a comfortable domesticity to slavery, indirectly signals the importance that race, social status and degrees of colour will have in the book to follow.

The Harper's 1899 edition of the book had an illustration of Roxy by E. W. Kemble apparently showing her as a stereotypical 'Aunt Jemima' figure in a domestic role (carrying a basket, and according to the picture's title, 'harvesting among the kitchens'). Her stout body is entirely covered in a plain white apron-dress, and she wears hooped ear-rings and a head-kerchief which completely conceals her hair. She is round-faced and thick-lipped and has coal-black features. This picture seems entirely in keeping with, indeed is conjured up by, the style and context of Roxy's speech. But such first impressions are completely misleading. The gap between the speech patterns Roxy shares with her larger slave community and her actual physical appearance confuses (or may even escape) the reader.[59] For the narrator then describes Roxy and draws attention to this disparity:

> From [her] manner of speech, a stranger would have expected her to be
> black, but she was not. Only one sixteenth of her was black, and that
> sixteenth did not show. She was of majestic form and stature . . . her
> gestures and movements distinguished by a noble and stately grace.
> Her complexion was very fair, with the rosy glow of vigorous health in
> the cheeks. . . . Her face was shapely, intelligent and comely – even
> beautiful.   (32)

In the discrepancy between expected African American stereotype and the
reality of this completely white, and beautiful woman, and in the way readerly
attention is drawn to it, Twain commences the challenge to conventional racial
(and racist) assumptions that will, for the most part, drive his book.

There is, though, a lack of transparency to this introductory scene. Or rather,
there are two different forms of transparency (speech and vision) which exist in
apparently contradictory relationship. But the reason for such contradiction,
and its importance, remains unexplained and opaque. The novel, throughout,
works through irony, subtlety, and indirection rather than through any direct
representation of authorial intent. The larger social meanings of such scenes and
incidents are veiled and difficult to penetrate. In both its narrative techniques
and in its overall composition, then, the book moves away from realism as Twain
(to borrow a word from Emily Dickinson) approaches his fictional themes
'aslant'.

The predominant tone of the novel, signalled by the selections from
'Pudd'nhead Wilson's Calendar' that form its chapter headings, is coolly cynical:

> *October* 12, *the Discovery*. It was wonderful to find America, but it would
> have been more wonderful to miss it.   (300)

> *April 1*. This is the day upon which we are reminded of what we are on
> the other three hundred and sixty-four.   (278)

Moreover, the use of a third-person and uninvolved narrator necessarily means
that the direct intimacy of Huck's first-person voice – and even the (rather
less-appealing) immediacy and fullness of expression of Hank Morgan's – are
missing here. Character here remains relatively undeveloped as Twain puts his
emphasis not on interiority (what his characters are thinking and feeling) but
on plot.

The overall bleakness of the novel is indicated in the way that the full representation of character, and of how a character chooses to act as he or she
negotiates the social world, is largely dismissed and ignored here. For character
is seen more as the slave of social circumstance rather than in negotiation with,
or in control of it. Three of the major 'characters' (Roxy, Tom Driscoll and

Valet de Chambre) end up disconnected from society. Roxy, broken-hearted and defeated, finally comforts herself with a narrow involvement in church affairs (301). Tom is sold down the river for the financial benefit of the creditors of the Percy Driscoll estate (302–3). Valet, 'rich and free' but speaking the language and with the manners of a slave, is alienated from both the free and slave worlds which compose this community, 'at peace nowhere but in the kitchen' (302). Only Pudd'nhead Wilson, who begins the novel as a marginalised figure, reverses this pattern to end as a fully-accepted member of the Dawson's Landing community. But, as I will show, that is hardly a matter for celebration.

The town of Dawson's Landing provides the backdrop and reference point to the novel's action, but many scenes and events take place on the margins of this community.[60] 'Pudd'nhead' Wilson, an outsider from New York State, is given his nickname on his very first day in the village, when he makes a dour joke that no one around him understands (I will return to this joke later). He lives on the 'extreme western verge of the town' with, following his 'deadly remark', no clients for his law firm (27). Only the occasional surveying and accountancy job – and his membership, with Judge Driscoll, in their two-person 'Society of Free-thinkers' (88) – binds him into the town's life. Many of the key scenes of the novel are, until the concluding sequences, enacted in secret or outside the framework of normal social life. Roxy, fearing that 'her child could grow up and be sold down the river' (41), swaps her 'black' baby (Valet), for her master's child (Tom), but tells no one of her act. She does later tell the boy now called 'Tom' (but in fact the real Valet) of his true status – 'You's a *nigger! – bawn* a nigger en a *slave!*' (113) – and of the identity of his father, Colonel Cecil Burleigh Essex. But this, too, occurs on the very western edge of town, in the 'haunted house', a two-storey log building and 'the last house in the town at that end' (112). And when the novel takes a melodramatic turn – as Tom kills Judge Driscoll, his supposed uncle and his present guardian, while attempting to rob him – this act, too, takes place out of the town's sight, and late at night.

Despite Tom's apparent social status, both he and Roxy are in fact outsiders, associated with criminal action, secrecy and disguise. Each of them, on a number of occasions, assume false identities. Roxy is freed on her first master's death, but is then treacherously sold back into slavery (downriver) by her son. Making her escape, she returns to town in black-face and cross-dress disguise, as a man in 'shabby old clothes' and 'show[ing] a black face and under an old slouch hat' (227). While Tom, who makes up his mind to rob Judge Driscoll when desperate for money (under pressure from Roxy, to re-buy her freedom), acts similarly – 'black[ing] his face with burnt cork' before the robbery, dressing in a 'suit of girl's clothes' (250) to make his escape. All such details and incidents move the reader away from the community centre to the subversive actions of a 'black' underclass that disrupt its stable life. The novel does constantly return us to ongoing town life – first with the story of the Italian twins and their reception, later with the murder trial. But it is in the plots and concealments that take place at the margins of the dominant white social world (but which affect its very core) that its emphasis and mainspring lies. Roxy and Tom provide a nightmare racial underside to the day-to-day comforts and contentment of Dawson's Landing, with Tom Driscoll playing a 'black-face' version of Indian Joe. In this novel, though, it is Driscoll who carries the main weight of the narrative interest rather than the Tom Sawyer equivalent, Pudd'nhead Wilson himself.

This emphasis on costume, cross-dressing, and blacking-up indicates the twinned nature of the novel's main themes – identity and race. Tom dresses as a woman, but is actually a man. Roxy reverses the process. Such disguise and performance necessarily raise the question of where 'authentic' identity lies. This question takes on an added charge where the subject of race is involved. I describe Tom as a black-face variant of Indian Joe. But he plays this role only in the southern racial imaginary (the town defines him as a 'black' slave where he is in fact, like his mother, absolutely white). He actually becomes that figure – a black murderer and thief – only momentarily as, like a performer in the minstrel-show (at the height of its popularity in the 1830s and 40s), he 'blacks-up' with the burnt cork.

Tom and Roxy are defined as 'black' courtesy of the southern legal codes that determine racial categorisation. A 'one-drop rule' (in place well into the twentieth century) meant that any offspring of a union between African-American and white was classed in the former racial category. The image of both Tom and his mother blacking up is then particularly resonant, for it draws our attention to the absurd nature of southern racial codes that literally (at least, in legal and social terms) make white into black. The central racial insight of the whole novel comes early on when the author describes Tom's mixed bloodlines – thirty-one parts white to one part black. It is the one-thirty-second black part that fixes his identity both as a slave and – these are the crucial words – 'by a fiction of law and custom a negro' (33). 'Blackness', the label that defines racial inferiority in the South, is, then, an entirely artificial 'fiction', a constructed category that bears no relation to actual human difference, and not even (necessarily) to the colour of one's skin.

Twain here reveals the fraudulence of socially-invented labels differentiating black from white, thus designating both superior and inferior status and who is a free man and who a slave. Such discriminatory classifications are reduced to idiocy as Twain shows that if you swap 'black' for 'white' no one can tell the difference. A Tweedledum and Tweedledee logic inhabits the text as Roxy swaps the two babies, 'Valet' accordingly becoming 'Tom', and the social order continues to function just as before. A child slave can change places with a representative of the best 'white' blood in the land – just as a pauper can change places with a prince – and, providing the switch of clothes goes unnoticed, there is apparently no way for them to be told apart.

Twain implies a further step here in the logic he establishes. For his exploration of racial being has a wider implication – that our notions of distinct identity (our 'essential' subjectivity or individual human difference) may be highly problematic, even completely illusory. For the differences between one individual and the next, he suggests, are not innate but kick-in from infancy as environment and conditioning affect being (something he also strongly argues in his later 'philosophical' work of 1906, *What is Man?*). Twain is raising a question here that is troubling to any reader – is there anything special inside me that makes my identity special and distinct? According to *Pudd'nhead Wilson's Calendar*, 'Training is everything. . . . [C]auliflower is nothing but cabbage with a college education' (67). Tom Driscoll, looked at in this light, is nothing but a slave with a Yale education. Just as the cauliflower appears as the cabbage (comically) fades from view, so Tom assumes 'Eastern polish' (68) as he leaves behind – from the very moment of Roxy's switch – the vulgarity and uncouth manners (302) of the slave. It is Valet (the 'real' Tom) who is defined by the latter qualities, entirely the product of his upbringing as a slave. And even when he is restored to his 'rightful' social place, he is unable ever to re-adjust to it.

There is, however, some problem with this reading, for – in Tom's representation – another and more complex element seems to enter the picture. Tom, we are informed, has a 'native viciousness' (59) and shows, on occasion, 'an evil light in his eye' (242). His mother, Roxy, claims that it is the 'one part nigger' (188) in him that makes him the coward that he is – and, to follow her logic, a bully, thief and murderer too. In other words, Tom's identity as a metaphorical cabbage (to return to the calendar entry above) remains visible and unchanging despite the cauliflower characteristics he has adopted. Such a reading makes it possible to argue that the book is confused in its racial politics. It interrogates the assumptions of the Southern system that makes race the marker of human difference and of social identity. But such a questioning then seems to be undermined by a counter-move that sees Tom's identity as natively vicious and evil, fixed at birth (nature not nurture) by his African American racial origins.

Throughout his work Twain would have problems with this nature-nurture opposition. In *Connecticut Yankee*, the comparison of 'that one microscopic atom in me that is truly *me*' with that 'training [which] is everything' raises the question of where the boundary between the two lies. Elsewhere, Twain allows the human subject far greater autonomy and agency than the first of those quotes suggests. So, for instance, the later determinist arguments in *What is Man?* cannot be reconciled with the acute moral indignation that continued to motivate much of his thought and writings, based on the assumption that human beings are not just conditioned by the circumstances of their lives but can – and must – act to change them. In Tom's case, however, it is possible to find a way around the nature-nurture contradiction and the racist implications that accompany the idea that his moral 'blackness' is assumed at birth. First, Roxy's words about her son's racially-inherited characteristics can be quickly dismissed as a clear result of the way she is herself affected by the racist ide-ology of the dominant white social world. Given that, Tom's viciousness still seems to set him apart from the town's other, and legitimate, *FFV*'s (Twain's satiric shorthand for the Southern version of an aristocracy, the First Families of Virginia). Twain's explanation that "Tom' was a bad baby, from the very beginning of his usurpation' (52) might lead us, though, to argue in a number of different ways. First, it could indicate that Tom is indeed innately vicious, but that viciousness may have nothing to do with his racial origins. Or, sec-ond, it may confirm Tom's viciousness but explain it – and its extreme form – as a *result* of his new upbringing and of what one critic calls 'the historical deterioration of aristocratic authority'.[61] This latter reading can be reinforced by referring to a passage from Twain's working notes for the novel. Alluding to Tom's refusal of the duel with Count Luigi, he wrote: 'what was high in [Tom] came from either blood, & was the monopoly of neither color; but that which was base was the white blood in him debased by the brutalising effects of a long-drawn heredity of slave-owning . . .'.[62] A third alternative which, though, applies just to his act of murder, is that Tom may *unconsciously* be acting out quite another racial part: as a justified avenger, paying back his guardian (and substitute father) for the past crimes committed by the white ruling-class, as a whole, against the African American race.

This brings me back to my earlier argument about the novel's apparent attack on any notion of 'essential' subjectivity: the belief that we each have an individual core to our selfhood that separates us off from those about us. As the similar-looking babies are swapped, each may become just what the other might have been. For it is possible that Valet, using the above argument about aristocratic authority and its deterioration, may have turned out just like Tom. This indicates the anxieties about identity which permeate the text and which extend beyond its racial confines. For the final question asked of the reader is just how – once we take away environmental circumstance and training – we can tell individuals apart: in this case, tell Tom from Valet.

The answer to this question brings us back to Pudd'nhead Wilson, the community outsider. It is his hobby of finger-printing that allows him to untangle the confusion of identity set in motion by Roxy's first actions. This hobby, too, allows him to solve the crime of murder on which the plot finally centres. But Wilson's scientific knowledge and intervention (sorting out who is who) actually help to confirm the problematic and insecure nature of individual and separate selfhood. For just as long as Roxy, the original perpetrator of the 'crime' of switching the boys, remains silent, the *only* way to tell Valet and Tom apart is through their fingerprints. Indeed, had Wilson not taken these prints in infancy, the identity mix-up could never have been resolved. Identity, in other words, is reduced in this novel to a minimal and physical form, to the lines on one's skin alone. Any notion of a distinct and separate selfhood of any real substance tends to collapse in such awareness.

Our (standard western) assumptions of selfhood as fixed, centred and stable, operating in an environment where personal agency and moral responsibility are the rule, are revealed in this novel to be illusory. Twain questions the fundamentals of such values and beliefs. There is one person, however, who seems to stand above such judgements. The dry irony, scientific skills and apparent ability (as a free-thinker) to step above social prejudice, of the title character, David (Pudd'nhead) Wilson, mark his early difference from those around him. And the joke that puzzles all bystanders, and leads to his election as pudd'nhead, in fact provides the metaphorical key to the novel's main theme. Hearing an invisible dog snarl and howl, he enters into dialogue with the citizens around him:

> 'I wish I owned half of that dog.'
> 'Why?' Somebody asked.
> 'Because I would kill my half'. (24)

This joke translates to Tom and Valet and the book's racial theme. In this southwestern community black and white stand in Siamese connection, twinned and inseparable, their stories inevitably interconnected. Tom (one half of that metaphorical dog) is finally silenced, effectively killed-off, as a result of his transgressive actions and the social threat they represent. His aggression is brutally tamed as he is sent down-river and his original status – as an owned object (a slave) – is re-established. But Valet too is left metaphorically dead. Trained as a slave, and able to speak only in an African American vernacular, he is incapable of re-taking his 'rightful' place as a community leader and as a scion of white 'aristocratic' manhood. The killing of one dog then effectively also kills the other. On a larger level, this works as a metaphor for the symbiotic nature of race relations in the South. In a social world where black and white exist in a twinned relationship, to kill one half of the dog (take away that half's freedom and political rights and to reduce it to the level of owned property alone) is necessarily to seal the fate of the other half. Such a society cannot survive healthily for very long. The final message of the allegory is that a community built on prejudice and racism carries within it the seeds of its own inevitable demise.

We should note here that, as in *Huckleberry Finn*, Twain may well have had his contemporary South in mind as he wrote, as well as the ante bellum region of the text's setting. For the problem of race remained pressing, as evidenced by the 1896 *Plessy* v. *Ferguson* Supreme Court case. Homer Plessy, seven-eighths white and one-eighth black, was jailed (in 1892) for breaking Louisiana segregation law whereby 'black' and 'white' were forbidden from travelling in the same railroad carriage. The Supreme Court validated the legality of this conviction. It is likely that this case cannot have been far from Twain's mind as he wrote.[63]

In my analysis of the 'half a dog' incident I elaborate considerably on Wilson's 'joke'. In doing so, however, I tend to reconstruct a definitive authorial viewpoint and to view the novel through present-day critical eyes. And if Wilson is associated here with the potential ability to step above the prejudices of his surroundings, this is not consistent with the developing narrative. For he becomes a changed figure and one who is apparently unable to see the full implications of his own early joke. Separated from the community at the book's start, he ends up accepted by it, an insider. He achieves this by proving Tom's guilt and by completely failing to acknowledge the deeper racial implications of the exchange of identities that has occurred. The novel switches into detective mode toward its conclusion and, as it does so, Wilson is linked to the conventional patterns of that genre – the restoration of the rule of law and of disrupted communal norms. The trial reveals that black and white can switch places without anyone being aware of the difference. But this – Roxy's first 'crime' – is subordinated to the more pressing crime in the town's eyes, the discovery of the identity of the Judge's killer. Tom is proved to be guilty, but, in an ironical twist, is not imprisoned but sold downriver, too valuable as the slave that he in fact is to be shut up for life (303).

Wilson, in other words, loses his prior independence as this sequence occurs. During the trial, he becomes the agent and hero of the community and apparently assumes its values. He restores what had been racially upset back to its 'proper' place. Valet's remaining uncouth presence gives the lie to any notion of complete and satisfactory closure, but this is something neither Pudd'nhead nor the community choose to emphasise. The basic problem that brings the whole story into being is that Valet has been able to become Tom (and vice-versa) without anyone knowing that this has happened. Yet what this suggests about the flawed racial foundations of this social world goes finally ignored. What counts here is the solution of the murder and Tom's punishment (though we should also note that Wilson does save a falsely accused man from imprisonment). Wilson's potential role as a sharp-sighted social critic effectively disappears as he leads the dramatic performance that the trial scene becomes; turns into yet another adult Tom Sawyer.

There is one further dimension of the novel that needs comment – its 'jack-leg' nature (311). Originally, Twain wrote, the novel on which he was working 'changed itself from a farce to a tragedy while I was going along with it'. As this happened, he realised that what he had in front of him was 'not one story, but two stories tangled together' (310). As Twain veered between generic extremes, a farcical story of Siamese twins seemed to take him in quite another direction than his 'tragedy' about race relations in the South. (Such moves are, in fact, typical of the swings within much of his late work. He wrote exuberant comedy like the 1902 story, 'A Double-Barreled Detective Story'. But, alongside, he produced disturbing dream tales of uncertain subjectivity, collapsing knowledge, and the loss of control over surrounding circumstances – like the 1898 'The Great Dark'.) In this case, Twain decided to split his novel in two, performing 'a kind of literary Caesarian operation' (310) and publishing *Those Extraordinary Twins* as a separate story in the same book (the original title of the American Publishing Company's first edition was *Pudd'nhead Wilson and Those Extraordinary Twins*).

While *Pudd'nhead Wilson* can be read independently, it is nonetheless revealing to read it alongside its textual partner. The somewhat problematic presence of Luigi and Angelo in *Pudd'nhead Wilson* is thereby in part explained, as are certain odd moments in the novel where the traces of the Siamese brothers of *Those Extraordinary Twins* remain clearly visible. Twain has high jinks in the latter book with this version of the 'phillipene' (323) Luigi and Angelo, their physical peculiarities, and their battles for authority as they each look to control their single body. Their Siamese connection and the scandal in nature they represent, both supplements and shadows the racial twinning (and scandal in culture) that occurs in *Pudd'nhead*. The impossibility of firmly distinguishing one twin from the other, when both exist in one joined body, reinforces, too, the theme of problematic identity in the sister novel. If both texts, then, do in

very notion of a fixed literary canon came under radical interrogation. This interrogation was in line with the new attention to cultural pluralism at that time, and the revision of literary studies to concentrate on types of writing – by African Americans, Native Americans, Latinos/as, Asian Americans, immigrant and regional writers, women, the working class etc. – marginalised or forgotten until that point. American literary history, in other words, was subject to re-accentuation, as critics looked not to celebrate 'great works' but instead to capture what Sacvan Bercovitch calls 'the heterogeneity [or variousness] of America'.[4] This critical agenda is still very much in place. So, for instance, the most recent (fifth) edition of the *Heath Anthology of American Literature* omits *Huckleberry Finn* from its Twain selection, prints only one very short story ('Hills Like White Elephants') and one chapter of *A Farewell to Arms* to represent Hemingway, while it includes nineteen poems under the title 'A Sheaf of Poetry by Late-Nineteenth-Century American Women'.

I see no problem at all (quite the opposite) with such a widening and democratisation of American literary studies, but would resist the flattening out of value judgements that can accompany it. In Chapter 2, I quoted Toni Morrison's 1996 introduction to *Adventures of Huckleberry Finn*, where she gives her reasons for judging the book 'classic literature'. While I would avoid that term, I am reluctant to abandon her way of thinking. I would not deny the political and cultural determinants that helped to produce the traditional literary canon, nor that literary values change over time and are dependent on the community of readers involved. But I would continue to argue that some works outweigh others in historical and aesthetic importance. And that, in their impact on succeeding generations, novels like *Huckleberry Finn* will be around, to amuse, please and intellectually engage their readers, for some time yet. For at least part of the distinctive quality of such texts is their ability to continue to release new meaning to the different historical readerships they engage. I illustrate something of this process as I continue.

That having been said, however, I would still look (metaphorically) to level the literary playing field somewhat in the direction suggested by Arac's critique. This would be to accept that, while *Huckleberry Finn* still remains one of the best-known and most stimulating of Twain's texts, the extreme emphasis that has been placed on it at the expense of his other works and that of other authors, needs some redress. Thus certainly in the last decades *Pudd'nhead Wilson* has begun to draw closer to Twain's earlier novel in the attention it has received. This is due to the recent intense re-exploration of American racial history and, accordingly, of the critical attention paid to the construction of 'whiteness' in America: to 'white racial identity both as a category of experience (what it means to be white in a multi-ethnic world) and as a mode of domination with its own languages and strategies'.[5] And, as I will shortly show, a recent interest in transnationalism has prompted a shift in attention in Twain criticism to the texts that best fit that agenda. And while *Huckleberry Finn* still gets its full share of attention, there is a new focus on what we might call its 'thick' literary context – how it connects and contrasts with the work of others writing in and around the same period: Harriet Beecher Stowe, George Washington Cable, Joel Chandler Harris, Paul Laurence Dunbar, W. E. B. DuBois, William Dean Howells, and others.

Increasing attention has also been given to the way in which previous generations of academics and intellectuals helped to construct an accepted literary canon in America in the first place. In the case of *Huckleberry Finn*, this has meant a renewed examination of the particular politics and value-systems of those who, in the past, gave the novel its 'classic' status. Thus Mencken's comments on Twain fitted entirely with his assault on Puritanism in America – his belief that a pervasive and inherited sense of sin had crippled the culture. It was part, too, of his celebration of the emergence of a powerful, independent and distinctively American literary tradition in his own time (and linked to his championship of Willa Cather, Theodore Dreiser, Sherwood Anderson, Sinclair Lewis, F. Scott Fitzgerald and others).

Jonathan Arac is more interested in the book's more recent history and traces *Huckleberry Finn*'s full 'hypercanonization' to the immediate post-World War Two period. His argument is detailed and complex and I cannot do it full justice here. He puts, though, particular emphasis on critic Lionel Trilling's influential 1948 reading of the novel. Trilling stressed the intensity of Huck's moral life and how his virtuous 'human heart' resisted the pressures of the 'outer world',[6] especially fore-grounding Chapter 31 of the novel: Huck's decision to 'go to hell' rather than reveal Jim's whereabouts to his legal owner. Arac argues that the internal conflict and 'great moral crisis' represented in this chapter tapped into Trilling's own particular cultural situation. As a liberal intellectual, he could not give his allegiance to the orthodox left-wing views of those critics and artists who had been writing in the 1930s, during the Great Depression. For the generation of the late 40s and 50s saw socialism as a movement crippled by its mechanical view of history and its downplaying of the individual imagination in favour of larger group solidarity. Nor could Trilling endorse the dulling and repressive tendencies of right wing conservatism, patterns that were becoming increasingly evident at this time.

Huck's position – caught between conforming to the surrounding social order (that Twain had shown to be corrupt) or following his own individual conscience – became, then, a mirror of Trilling's own view of the world and position in it. The complex individual self and his (in this case) imaginative moral sensibility become here the sole site of value. This exactly fitted Trilling's own need (as an intellectual) to pursue an independent course outside the scan either of rigid party loyalty or of respectable and conventional conformity. His own, essentially political, move to the practice and praise of an 'anti-Communist liberal imagination' was in complete accord with his reading of Twain's book.[7] This interpretation of the novel, and the emphasis necessarily placed on a few key textual moments, would determine (Arac suggests) the critical response of a whole generation of readers.

Present-day critics have come – as cultural agendas have changed – to focus on different aspects of the novel. Trilling's emphasis on independent moral character has been challenged by more recent understandings of Huck's self-hood as deeply enmeshed within, and formed by, the verbal structures and value systems of the world through which he moves. For the very way Huck thinks and the words he uses are largely structured by the south-western social order that (just about) contains him. There has been much more emphasis, then, on Huck's social conditioning and on a struggle for independent action that is only partially successful – for even his decision to 'go to hell' is, initially at least, a decision not to act: not to send Miss Watson that crucial letter. This has been accompanied by an interrogation of the apparently rigid oppositions that for so long provided the key to (mythic) readings of the text: the river and the raft with its 'community of saints' on board versus the riverbank world and the corrupt civilisation inhabiting it. More attention is now paid to the blurring of such oppositions: the way in which these two apparently opposed spatial and symbolic worlds are in fact bound in an unbreakable connection.

But – and we might expect this, given the move toward cultural pluralism and the challenge to white male authority of recent years – most recent debate about the novel has focused on race. I explore the way that this has affected readerly understandings of Jim's role in the novel in Chapter 3. I also show there how the novel has been reinterpreted and given a new historical emphasis by the exploring of its racial meanings in terms of the post Civil War period in which Twain wrote (rather than the ante bellum period when the novel is set). The most intense debate, however and one inspired by an increasingly critical African American readership, has focused on the repeated use of the word 'nigger' in the book. The use of this most-demeaning term of abuse has led to accusations that the book itself is 'racist trash',[8] and to legal challenges over the book's classroom use.

While such concerns are understandable, to dismiss the novel on this basis would be unfortunate. Twain would never completely escape the racial stereo-typing that remained so prevalent in his period. But his words and actions speak loudly of his increasing hatred for slavery and its legacies. He provided financial support for Warner T. McGuinn, one of the first African American students to attend Yale Law School, writing to the School Dean (in December 1885) that: 'We have ground the manhood out of them [African Americans], & the shame is ours, not theirs, & we should pay for it'.[9] In 1901, he would write (but not publish) 'The United States of Lyncherdom', an attack on the 'epidemic of bloody insanities' taking place in the South in the post-Reconstruction years (*TSSE2*, 486). And in *Huckleberry Finn*, his anti-racist message and intentions are equally clear. Indeed much of the novel seems to turn on the use, by Huck and others, of a word which was the absolute norm in the south-western social world of the time, and its complete failure to provide the measure of Jim's identity and human value. To accuse Twain of racism for highlighting and interrogating both the word and its function seems then a fundamental misreading of the book.

There are multiple instances (of which I give just two for illustrative purposes) of how this interrogation works. Pap rants against the government for allowing a 'free nigger . . . from Ohio; a mulatter, most as white as a white man . . . a p'fessor in a college' to vote. He continues:

> Thinks I, what is the country a-coming to? It was 'lection day, and I was just about to go and vote, myself, if I warn't too drunk to get there; but when they told me there was a State in this country where they'd let that nigger vote, I drawed out. I says I'll never vote agin. (49–50)

The satiric intent could not be clearer. This African American is more or less as 'white' as pap himself, and is certainly cleaner, smarter, and better-educated. Pap's decision to withdraw his (drunken) vote is clearly as advantageous to the political health of the nation as the college professor's decision to use his. Similarly, late in the novel, when the doctor praises Jim for staying at Tom's wounded side, he praises him 'because he ain't a bad nigger . . . I never see a nigger that was a better nuss or faithfuller. . . . I tell you, gentleman, a nigger like that is worth a thousand dollars' (356–7). The words ring with irony. To value Jim as property while to praise him for his human worth (his caring loyalty) indicts the slave-system as it gives the lie to the supposed inferiority of African Americans. Indeed through the novel Jim stands as an indicator of the generosity, selflessness and affection that the white social world consistently lacks.

The problem still remains of using in the classroom a book that repeatedly uses such a racially charged word, and which relies on irony for its effect. Such irony requires the recognition that neither Pap or the doctor's words are to be taken at face value but are deliberately introduced to satirise racist assumptions. Careful teaching, the use of historical background materials, and of other relevant literary texts (*The Narrative of the Life of Frederick Douglass*, for instance) can help to find a way around such problems.[10] And when this same term is commonly used within the African American community as a hard-edged and streetwise signifier of masculinity and of insider 'authenticity' (however many in that community might disapprove of the fact), any move to ban Twain's book for the repeated use of this same word cannot help but take on a strange look.

Adventures of Huckleberry Finn, then, is likely to remain an important novel in American (and global) culture and – as long as racial difference is the mark of prejudice and inequality – with good cause. In the past, the novel has also tended to be read in the context of a celebratory American exceptionalism – the idea of a single national narrative significantly different from (and better than) that of other nations. So the Huck of the novel's ending, who 'light[s] out for the Territory ahead of the rest' (366), can figure as the representative American alone in the wilderness world – ready to cast off the past and make a new and self-reliant start, depending for his guide on the authority of individual conscience rather than of inherited social convention. But the novel (as I suggest above) is more likely now to be read in terms of the various power relations – class, regional and racial – which have marked and still mark, American culture. Such relationships, and the tensions and pressures they produce, also play an important role (in their different ways) in the book's global reception. As I say this, however, it is important to remember two things. First, we must keep in mind the interpretative shifts and the making of unexpected connections that will inevitably occur as the book is read and interpreted by an international audience and in that different historical and cultural context. And second, we should accept that there remains something about the oppositions that structure the novel – black and white, instinct and impulse and social belonging and learned language, river and shore, raft and permanent 'home', civilisation and wilderness, child and adulthood, male and female, slavery and freedom – which (however unstable they turn out to be on close examination) continue to give the novel a certain mythic resonance and appeal.

Twain criticism has diversified in recent years, partly in line with an increasing awareness of the multiple and fragmented nature of American culture(s). *Connecticut Yankee* now tends to be read as a text that challenges any in-built belief in the superiority of that culture and its values, which offers a sharp critique of both the progressive historical assumptions and the colonialist mentality of the late nineteenth-century American (and western) world. In *No. 44, The Mysterious Stranger* (written between 1902 and 1908 but based on earlier unfinished manuscripts), the magical stranger of the title, who is known only as '44', at one point reverses time and history. He shows August Feldner, the first-person narrator, a sequence of funerals being held over again, and of hearses and funeral processions 'marching solemnly backwards'. This is followed by a vision of 'yesterday's battles . . . being refought, wrong-end-first' with 'the previously killed . . . getting killed again'. 44 then stages an 'Assembly of the Dead' where 'for hours and hours the dead passed by in continental masses, and the bone-clacking was so deafening you could hardly hear yourself think'. This procession goes back to Noah and to Adam's predecessors, even including the 'under-sized skeleton' of 'the Missing Link' itself (*MS*, 400–3). Twain, here, again dismembers progressive notions of an evolutionary development to human history by replaying it front to back. Thus 'the apparent normality of the parade, the popular expression of mass spectacle in America', is undermined as Twain suggests that conventional celebrations of human events are a grotesque mistruth, and that a 'parade of regress and not progress' may better represent history's narrative. This parade is one of repeated and re-enacted death rather than of ongoing and improving life.[11]

Of Twain's other works, *Puddn'head Wilson* now gets almost as much attention as *Huckleberry Finn* for its deep engagement with the problem of America and race. *Which Was It?* – a late narrative eventually published in its unfinished form in 1968 – has been the subject of new interest for that same reason. Recent books on Twain's sexual politics as revealed through the courtship of his wife-to-be, on masculinity, race and class identity and on Twain's role as a professional writer and publisher in the fast-changing, late-nineteenth-century literary market, are just some of the newer critical directions that have been taken.[12]

Most recently, an increasing attention has been paid to Twain's status as a writer whose work spans national categories, with particular emphasis on the travel book and the anti-imperialist writings of his late years. I suggest in Chapter 3 that the fact that Twain spent so much time abroad – especially in Europe, but also in the wider international arena – and wrote extensively about other nations and cultures, is likely to make him a key figure in the strongly transnational critical turn of recent years.[13] I extend my earlier and very brief working definition of transnationalism here. While it is inappropriate in an introductory book to do more than outline the contours of this subject, some mention of this development in the critical field is necessary.

By transnationalism, we mean the cultural intersections and exchanges that take place between nations, and the way we can then read American Literature, and (in this case) Twain's writing in particular, as composed of a series of negotiations between national and international spaces.[14] But the term refers, too, to the challenge to the concept of nationhood itself. For we live now in a period of globalisation, at a time when the whole notion of independent national units separated from one another by firmly defined cultural and geopolitical boundaries has been accordingly weakened. (This is not, though, to deny the continued power and importance of nationalism, as events in America post 9/11 clearly illustrate.) In line with the increasing emphasis on such global understandings of culture, transnationalism looks to approach national literatures in a different way. Rather than focusing on what makes the literature of a specific country identifiably 'English' or 'American' (for example), it sets such different (national) cultural formations against each other both to illuminate the strengths, limits and selective blindnesses of each, and to emphasise the interrelationship between them.

In doing this four related things can happen. First, the nature of the contacts between different countries and their cultures, and their differences, conflicts and inequalities, can be explored. Second, as we examine such cross-border relations, we can identify the ways in which cultural borrowings and interchanges occur – how any one national culture is not a privileged and self-contained space, but rather a fusion of all kinds of influences, many of which come from elsewhere. Third, to examine one national formation by setting it in a broader international context allows us to ask questions about, and thus loosen any unthinking acceptance of, the ideological assumptions and power relationships (and their justices and injustices) of that nation. Lastly, in revealing the outlines and limitations of a particular nation-state and the way it functions in this way, we can look – where this may be appropriate – to challenge its claims to domination and authority over its citizens' lives.

I recognise that this is all very abstract. And the impact of this form of criticism on studies of Mark Twain's work is at present relatively slight. I bring something of this perspective to my chapter on Twain's early travel writings. At a denser and more complex level, there are a number of recent book chapters and essays that approach Twain in this way.[15] Here, I briefly focus on the last 1897 travel book, *Following the Equator*, to illustrate – on a small scale, but in more concrete terms – how a transnational approach might operate.[16]

In Chapter 5 of *Following the Equator* Twain comments on the (western) naming of the constellations and how inappropriate this can be. The 'Southern Cross,' for instance, is unrecognisable from its descriptive name. He then makes a more general comment on the relation between imperialist activity and the tendency to re-name things in a possessive way:

In a little while, now – I cannot tell exactly how long it will be – the globe will belong to the English-speaking race; and of course the skies also. Then the constellations will be re-organized, and polished up, and re-named – the most of them 'Victoria,' I reckon. . . . Several towns and things, here and there, have been named for Her Majesty already.   (80)

Twain uses his role as traveller here, and the comparative view it allows, clearly to satirise the proprietary sense and assumption of superiority and authority (not just over settled territory, but of the furthest limits of the natural horizon too) of his own home western culture.

Indeed, throughout the book and despite his inconsistencies – for there are inconsistencies here[17] – Twain's comments on the countries that he visits serve to reflect back on his own country's history, most particularly on its racial practices.[18] Sometimes such reflection appears to operate at a conscious level, but sometimes unconsciously. The former seems to be the case when he describes the behaviour of 'the white man' with his 'appliances of civilization' toward the aborigine 'savages' in Australia, and the policy of selective 'extermination' used. Twain then generalises:

In more than one country we have hunted the savage and his little children and their mother with dogs and guns through the woods and swamps for an afternoon's sport. . . . In many countries we have taken the savage's land from him, and made him our slave, and lashed him every day, and broken his pride, and made death his only friend. . . . (207–12)

America is never mentioned here, but this passage cannot be read without both American Indian and African American history springing immediately to mind. Caught in the folds of Twain's description of his global travel lies, then, a very American racial theme.

Similarly, Twain reverses routine assumptions concerning colour and the symbolic hierarchies they connote as he comments on the native populace in both India and South Africa. In the West, whiteness (normally associated with the angelic) is generally privileged over blackness. But when he comments on his time abroad, Twain contrasts 'the splendid black satin skin of the South African Zulus of Durban', and the beauty of 'nearly all [the] black and brown skins' he sees around him in India, with 'the bleached-out, unwholesome, and sometimes frankly ghastly' look of the 'white complexion' (381). Given Twain's contemporary (white) American audience, this is striking material. In the America of the 1890s, whites largely only had eyes for each other and had once more consigned the African American population – particularly in the South – to diminished social status and civil rights. In contrasting the attractions of the black body with a white ugliness, Twain both undermines conventional western aesthetics and at least hints toward a larger moral and political upsetting of standard racial and racist assumptions (as we, for instance, remember the link between Pap Finn's 'fish-belly white' skin in *Huckleberry Finn* and the ignorant prejudice of his politics), both on an international and national (American) scale. Indeed, the more general picture of white and non-white interaction in the book often appears to endorse such a reversal.

At such points throughout the book – most noticeably in scenes like those mentioned in Chapter ,2 where the cuffing of a native servant in India mentally returns Twain to slavery and his Missouri childhood – we see, and in more intense form, an effect to which I earlier referred. Writing on *Innocents Abroad* (in Chapter 3), I suggested how complete disorientation can sometimes occur when American and foreign experiences are brought together. And when this happens, it can lead to a radical re-visioning of assumptions and ways of seeing that are taken for granted within an American national context. This is exactly the type of thing that occurs in all these cases in *Following the Equator*. Transnational interchange provides a clear means, at this later stage of Twain's career, for raising challenging questions about the shape and direction of his own national culture.

We see something of the same process in Twain's late non-fiction writings too, the form his work increasingly took. Twain remained a prolific writer until late in his life. He spent a great deal of time working on his autobiography (still unpublished in its entirety), but he wrote fiction too, much of it exploring the problematic boundary between dream life and reality, and much of it unpublished. Other such work veered wildly between an ironic pessimism and bleak determinism, and forms of humour that could be both surreal and anarchic. But he increasingly wrote non-fiction. As close to a global celebrity as one could get in his period, much of his most effective writing was satiric and exploited the crossovers between national and international targets. He attacked what he would call 'The Blessings-of-Civilization Trust' (*TSSE2*, 461), as he became increasingly opposed to colonising ventures and imperialist practices – as carried out both by the American government (especially in the Phillipines) and by foreign powers. He accordingly became a powerful international voice representing the anti-imperialist movement. US Imperialism – 'the multiple histories of overseas expansion, conquest, conflict, and resistance which have shaped the cultures of the United States and the cultures of those it has doiminated within and beyond its geopolitical boundaries' – is a key concern for present-day transnationalists.[19] In essays like 'To the Person Sitting in Darkness' (1901) and 'The War Prayer' (1905), Twain anticipated such concerns, providing sharp critiques of international colonial conquest and of the national and international mind-frame – the patriotic oratory, religious militarism and greedy harvesting of material gain – that supported it. His considered judgement on the American role in the Spanish-American war was that 'we have gone there to conquer, not to redeem' (*New York Herald*, 15 October 1900), a statement that has some resonance at a time of renewed (and nationalistic) American military interventions overseas. Given the latter circumstances, we can expect this part of his writings to be of increasing critical interest in the immediate future. Twain retains his ability to speak meaningfully both to his countrymen and women and to an international audience even as the centennial of his death approaches.

Notes

1 Mark Twain's life

1. Ron Powers, *Dangerous Water: A Biography of the Boy who Became Mark Twain* (New York: Basic Books, 1999) p. 218.
2. Henry Nash Smith's term in *Mark Twain: The Development of a Writer* (Cambridge, Mass.: Belknap Press, 1962) p. 72.
3. Shelley Fisher Fishkin, *Lighting out for the Territory: Reflections on Mark Twain and American Culture* (New York: Oxford University Press, 1997) p. 111.
4. Terrell Dempsey, *Searching for Jim: Slavery in Sam Clemens's World* (Columbia, Missouri: University of Missouri Press, 2003) pp. 52–4, 222–4, 281.
5. See, most recently, Andrew Dix, 'Twain and the Mississippi'. In Peter Messent and Louis J. Budd (eds.), *Companion to Mark Twain* (Oxford, Blackwell: 2005) pp. 293–308.
6. For a detailed exploration of the Olivia Langdon-Twain relationship see Susan K. Harris, *The Courtship of Olivia Langdon and Mark Twain* (Cambridge: Cambridge University Press, 1996).
7. Quoted in Jennifer L. Zaccara, 'Mark Twain, Isabel Lyon, and the "Talking Cure": negotiating nostalgia and nihilism in the *Autobiography*'. In Laura E. Skandera Trombley and Michael J. Kiskis (eds.), *Constructing Mark Twain: New Directions in Scholarship* (Columbia: University of Missouri Press, 2001) p. 105.
8. Ibid., p. 121.
9. Hamlin Hill, *Mark Twain: God's Fool* (New York: Harper & Row, 1967), pp. xxvii and 273.
10. Karen Lystra, *Dangerous Intimacy: The Untold Story of Mark Twain's Final Years* (Berkeley: University of California Press, 2004) pp. 60 and 132.
11. Ibid., p. 100.
12. Ibid., p. 246.

2 Contexts

1. Toni Morrison, 'Introduction', *Adventures of Huckleberry Finn*. The Oxford Mark Twain (see introductory 'Notes on Referencing'), pp. xxxi and xli.

2. Figures from Kevin MacDonnell, 'The primary first editions of Mark Twain', *Firsts: The Book Collector's Magazine*, Vol. 8, No. 7/8 (July/August 1998) pp. 33, 35, 39, and 'Huck Finn among the issue-mongers', *Firsts*, Vol. 8, No. 9 (Sept. 1998), p. 29. And from Ron Powers, *Mark Twain: A Life* (New York: Free Press, 2005) pp. 489–90.

3. See Steven Mailloux, 'Cultural reception and social practices'. In *Rhetorical Power* (Ithaca: Cornell University Press, 1989) pp. 100–129.

4. Vonnegut refers to 'Incident in the Phillipines', published posthumously in 1924. See http://www.commondreams.org/views03/0514-05.htm

5. Henry Adams. *The Education of Henry Adams* (New York: The Modern Library, 1931 [1918]) p. 53.

6. Who is nonetheless still a fictional persona and does not necessarily represent the real Samuel Clemens.

7. We can connect this nightmare vision with what we now call 'abjection' – a focus on physical vulnerability, the rending and (in this case) the de-fleshing of the human body. Such concerns suggest larger anxieties about the status of the subject and its authority and autonomy: a topic worth pursuing in the larger body of Twain's writings.

8. And see Susan Gillman, *Blood Talk: American Race Melodramas and the Culture of the Occult* (Chicago: University of Chicago Press, 2003) pp. 120, 133–4.

9. Ron Powers, *Dangerous Water: A Biography of the Boy who Became Mark Twain* (New York: Basic Books, 1999) pp. 261, 272.

3 Works

1. Artemus Ward, *Complete Works* (London: Chatto & Windus, 1905) p. 79.

2. Quoted in Norris Yates, *The American Humorist: Conscience of the Twentieth Century* (Ames: Iowa State University Press, 1964) p. 11.

3. Quoted in Fred Kaplan, *The Singular Mark Twain* (New York: Doubleday, 2003) p. 136.

4. Shelley Fisher Fishkin, *Lighting out for the Territory: Reflections on Mark Twain and American Culture* (New York: Oxford University Press, 1997) p. 7.

5. See most recently: Larzer Ziff, *Return Passages: Great American Travel Writing 1780–1910* (New Haven: Yale University Press, 2000) and Jeffrey Alan Melton, *Mark Twain, Travel Books, and Tourism: The Tide of a Great Popular Movement* (Tuscaloosa: University of Alabama Press, 2002).

6. Patrick Holland and Graham Huggins, *Tourists with Typewriters: Critical Reflections on Contemporary Travel Writing* (Ann Arbor: University of Michigan Press, 2000 [1998]) p. 2; and James Buzard, *The Beaten Track: European Tourism. Literature and the Ways to 'Culture', 1800–1918* (Oxford: Clarendon, 1993) p. 2.

7. Henry James, *The American* (New York: W.W. Norton, 1978) p. 17.

8. My thanks to Alexis Haynes for his comments on the draft version of this chapter and for suggesting the importance of the Bellagio passage.

9. Richard Bridgman, *Traveling in Mark Twain*, (Berkeley: University of California Press, 1987) p. 9.
10. James Buzard, *The Beaten Track*, p. 11.
11. Ibid., p. 90.
12. Larzer Ziff, *Return Passages*, p. 22. Ziff's interpretative position differs from mine.
13. John F. Sears, *Sacred Places: American Tourist Attractions in the Nineteenth Century* (New York: Oxford University Press, 1989) p. 158.
14. Ibid., cit., p. 157.
15. Elisha P. Douglass, *The Coming of Age of American Business: Three Centuries of Enterprise, 1600–1900* (Chapel Hill: University of North Carolina Press, 1971) p. 389.
16. Andrew Dix, 'Twain and the Mississippi'. In Peter Messent and Louis J. Budd (eds.), *Companion to Mark Twain*, p. 297.
17. Howard Horwitz, *By the Law of Nature: Form and Value in Nineteenth-Century America* (New York: Oxford University Press, 1991) p. 111.
18. Gregg Camfield, 'A Republican artisan in the court of king capital: Mark Twain and commerce'. In Shelley Fisher Fishkin (ed.), *A Historical Guide to Mark Twain* (New York: Oxford University Press, 2002) p. 113.
19. Andrew Dix, 'Twain and the Mississippi', p. 296. I follow Dix's line of argument in this final section of my analysis.
20. Ibid., p. 298.
21. See Ron Powers, *Mark Twain: A Life*, p. 89.
22. Lee Clark Mitchell, 'Introduction' to Mark Twain, *The Adventures of Tom Sawyer* (Oxford: Oxford University Press [World's Classics], 1993) p. x.
23. http://etext.virginia.edu/railton/tomsawye/nostalgia/nostalgiahp. html
24. E. Anthony Rotundo, 'Boy culture: middle-class boyhood in nineteenth-century America'. In Mark C. Carnes and Clyde Griffen (eds.), *Meanings for Manhood: Constructions of Masculinity in Victorian America* (Chicago: University of Chicago Press, 1990) pp. 19 and 16.
25. Michael Oriard, *Sporting with the Gods: The Rhetoric of Play and Game in American Culture* (Cambridge: Cambridge University Press, 1991) p. 394.
26. See especially, Cynthia Griffin Wolff, '*The Adventures of Tom Sawyer*: A nightmare vision of American boyhood', *Massachusetts Review*, Vol. 21, No. 4 (Winter 1980) pp. 91–105.
27. Judith Fetterly, 'The sanctioned rebel', *Studies in the Novel*, Vol. 3 (Fall 1971) pp. 293–304.
28. Cynthia Griffin Wolff, '*The Adventures of Tom Sawyer*,' p. 94.
29. Lee Clark Mitchell, for instance, talks of 'the battle of discursive modes' within the book. 'Introduction', p. xxvi.
30. The first part of Twain's manuscript for *Huckleberry Finn* was rediscovered in 1990. The complete manuscript is now available in CD Rom form (*Huck Finn: The Complete Buffalo & Erie County Public Library Manuscript – Teaching and Research Digital Edition*, 2003) and is invaluable in adding to our understanding of the composition process of the book.

31. Gavin Jones notes: 'the shadow of Sut's language is thrown across the whole novel [*Huckleberry Finn*], not in a regionally specific sense but in a broader thematic concern with the links between social class and literacy, between educational level and ethical outlook'. 'Twain, language, and the Southern humorists.' In Peter Messent and Louis J. Budd (eds.), *Companion to Mark Twain*, p. 136.

32. http://docsouth.unc.edu/harrisg/gharris.html#Text.

33. Richard Brodhead, quoted in Peter Messent, 'Discipline and punishment in *The Adventures of Tom Sawyer*,' *Journal of American Studies*, Vol. 32, No. 2 (August 1998) p. 233. This is opposed to the physical punishments of *Tom Sawyer*.

34. Quoted in Peter Messent, *New Readings of the American Novel: Narrative Theory and its Application* (Houndmills, Macmillan, 1990) p. 217.

35. Peter Messent and Steve Courtney (eds.), *The Civil War Letters of Joseph Hopkins Twichell: A Chaplain's Story* (Athens: Georgia University Press, 2006) p. 46.

36. Christopher Gair, 'Whitewashed exteriors: Mark Twain's imitation whites', *Journal of American Studies*, Vol. 39, No. 2 (August 2005) p. 188.

37. W. E. B. DuBois, *The Souls of Black Folk* (New York: Norton, 1999 [1903]) p. 5.

38. Though any completely objective representation, or re-presentation, of reality is impossible. For a fuller discussion of this topic, see Peter Messent, 'Mark Twain, William Dean Howells, and realism'. In Peter Messent and Louis J. Budd (eds.), *Companion to Mark Twain*, pp. 186–208.

39. Quoted, ibid., p. 187.

40. Gavin Jones, 'Twain, language, and the Southern humorists', p. 134.

41. Shelley Fisher Fishkin, *Was Huck Black? Mark Twain and African-American Voices* (New York: Oxford University Press: 1993) pp. 49, 140.

42. David L. Smith, 'Huck, Jim, and American racial discourse'. In James S. Leonard, Thomas A. Tenney, and Thadious M. Davis (eds.), *Satire or Evasion? Black Perspectives on Huckleberry Finn* (Durham: Duke University Press, 1992) p. 112.

43. Shelley Fisher Fishkin, 'Mark Twain and race', in Fishkin (ed.), *A Historical Guide to Mark Twain*, p. 154.

44. Quoted in Eric Foner, *Reconstruction: America's Unfinished Revolution, 1863–1877* (New York: Harper and Row, 1989 [1988]) p. 602.

45. Ibid., p. 598.

46. Shelley Fisher Fishkin, *Was Huck Black?*, p. 75.

47. Christine MacLeod, 'Telling the truth in a tight place: *Huckleberry Finn* and the reconstruction era', *Southern Quarterly*, Vol. 34, No. 1 (Fall 1995) p. 7.

48. Susan K. Harris, 'Mark Twain and gender'. In Shelley Fisher Fishkin (ed.), *A Historical Guide to Mark Twain*, p. 186.

49. Though for the immediate period only, for 'before and after *Yankee* he was an enthusiastic Anglophile'. T. J. Lustig, 'Twain and modernity.' In Peter Messent and Louis J. Budd (eds.), *Companion to Mark Twain*, p. 88.

50. Ibid., pp. 82–3, 86. I follow Lustig closely here.

51. See ibid., pp. 83–4.

52. See Maria Ornella Marotti, *The Duplicating Imagination: Twain and the Twain Papers* (University Park: Philadelphia State University Press, 1990) p. 46.
53. Cindy Weinstein, *The Literature of Labor and the Labors of Literature: Allegory in Nineteenth-Century American Fiction* (Cambridge: Cambridge University Press, 1995) p. 10.
54. See also on this subject, Werner Sollors, 'Ethnicity'. In Frank Lentricchia and Thomas McLaughlin (eds.), *Critical Terms for Literary Study* (Chicago: University of Chicago Press, 1990) pp. 288–305.
55. Michael Davitt Bell, *The Problem of American Realism: Studies in the Cultural History of a Literary Idea* (Chicago: University of Chicago Press, 1993) p. 66.
56. T. J. Lustig, 'Twain and modernity', p. 91.
57. See Susan K. Harris, 'Mark Twain and America's Christian mission abroad'. In Peter Messent and Louis J. Budd (eds.), *Companion to Mark Twain*, p. 38.
58. Richard S. Lowry, *'Littery Man': Mark Twain and Modern Authorship* (New York: Oxford University Press, 1996) p. 7.
59. Though, in fact, not Kemble himself. Comparison with his later illustration of Roxy, appearing in the American Publishing Company's 1899 de luxe edition of Twain's work (but not the Harper's edition) reveals that, in the earlier illustration, she is not in fact the central figure represented but another and much less prominent figure and of lighter complexion. See Railton for commentary on this whole rather odd business: http//etext.lib.virginia-edu/railton/wilson/pwillshp.html.
60. My ideas here were stimulated by a conference paper given by Paula Harrington, 'Dawson's Landing: on the disappearance of domesticity in a slave-holding town', now published in The *Mark Twain Annual* 3 (2005) pp. 91–97.
61. John Carlos Rowe, *Through the Custom-House: Nineteenth-Century Fiction and Modern Theory* (Baltimore: Johns Hopkins University Press, 1982) p. 156.
62. Quoted in Shelley Fisher Fishkin, 'Race and culture at the century's end: a social context for *Pudd'nhead Wilson.*' *Essays in Arts and Sciences*, Vol. 19 (May 1990) p. 16.
63. And see Eric J. Sundquist, *To Wake the Nations: Race in the Making of American Literature* (Cambridge, Mass.: Belknap Press, 1993) pp. 225–70.

4 Critical reception and the late works

1. I borrow the words from Louis J. Budd.
2. H. L. Mencken, Review of Albert Bigelow Paine, *Mark Twain, A Biography*, *The Smart Set* (February 1913). William H. Nolte (ed.), *H. L. Mencken's Smart Set Criticism* (Washington D.C.: Regnery Gateway, 1987) p. 179.
3. Jonathan Arac, *Huckleberry Finn as Idol and Target: The Functions of Criticism in Our Time* (Madison: University of Wisconsin Press, 1997) pp. 11 and 133.

4. Sacvan Bercovitch and Myra Jehlen, *Ideology and Classic American Literature* (Cambridge: Cambridge University Press, 1986) p. 438.

5. Richard S. Lowry, 'Mark Twain and whiteness'. In Peter Messent and Louis J. Budd (eds.), *Companion to Mark Twain*, pp. 54–5.

6. See Jonathan Arac, *Huckleberry Finn as Idol and Target*, p. 120. See, too, Chapter 3.

7. See ibid., pp. 128, 130.

8. John H. Wallace, 'The Case Against *Huck Finn*.' In James S. Leonard *et al.* (eds.), *Satire or Evasion?*, p. 16.

9. Quoted in Shelley Fisher Fishkin, *Lighting Out for the Territory*, p. 101.

10. And see Jocelyn Chadwick-Joshua, *The Jim Dilemma: Reading Race in Huckleberry Finn* (Jackson: University Press of Mississippi, 1998).

11. See Hilton Obenzinger, 'Better dreams: political satire and Twain's final "Exploding" novel', *Arizona Quarterly* Vol. 61, No. 1 (Spring 2005) p. 180.

12. See Susan K. Harris, *The Courtship of Olivia Langdon and Mark Twain*; Randall Knoper, *Acting Naturally: Mark Twain in the Culture of Performance* (Berkeley: University of California Press, 1995); Richard S. Lowry, *'Littery Man': Mark Twain and Modern Authorship*.

13. Many other American writers too, from Cooper and Hawthorne onward, similarly spent significant periods abroad. This signals both a larger realisation of the gains to literature from cosmopolitanism, and that 'America' itself could best be understood comparatively.

14. For critical work in this area, see, for instance, Amy Kaplan, ' "Left alone with America": the absence of empire in the study of American culture'. In Amy Kaplan and Donald E. Pease (eds.), *Cultures of United States Imperialism* (Durham: Duke University Press, 1993) pp. 3–21; Paul Giles, 'Transnationalism and classic American literature', *PMLA*, Vol. 118, No. 1 (2003) pp. 62–77; and John Carlos Rowe, 'Nineteenth-century United States literary culture and transnationality', *PMLA*, Vol.118, No.1 (2003) pp. 78–89. My approach here follows Giles closely.

15. See, for instance, Amy Kaplan's analysis of Twain's early writing about native culture and colonialism in Hawaii in 'The imperial routes of Mark Twain'. In *The Anarchy of Empire in the Making of U.S. Culture* (Cambridge, Mass.: Harvard University Press, 2002) pp. 51–91; and John Carlos Rowe's 'Mark Twain's critique of globalization (old and new) in *Following the Equator, A Journey Round the World*', *Arizona Quarterly*, Vol. 61, No. 1 (Spring 2005) pp. 109–35. The content of Twain's work, not just in the travel books, but in many of his late writings, encourages such transnational readings.

16. In my earlier section on travel writing I focus primarily on US–European relations. Here, there is a different western/'other' dynamic. As America became a world power and imperialism took on international dimensions, so previous debates about national identity and culture were occluded.

17. Twain undoubtedly sometimes looks at the countries he travels through with ethnocentric eyes and he applauds colonial rule in India's case. See John Carlos Rowe

(above) and Peter Messent, 'Racial and colonial discourse in *Following the* Equator', *Essays in Arts and Sciences*, Vol. 22 (October 1993) 67–83.

18. Amy Kaplan suggests that transnationalism 'relat[es] . . . internal [American] categories of gender, race, and ethnicity to the global dynamics of Empire building', 'Left alone with America', p. 16. This is exactly what Twain does in his book.

19. Amy Kaplan, 'Left alone with America', p. 4.

Guide to further reading

There have been a huge number of books written on and about Mark Twain. This is a subjective and highly selective list of some of the biographical, bibliographical and critical studies available – one that is aimed at the undergraduate reader. Only books wholly devoted to Twain are included. For a survey of some recent trends in Twain criticism, see Chapter 4.

Biography

Hill, Hamlin. *Mark Twain: God's Fool.* New York: Harper & Row, 1973. Provocative reading of Twain's late years focusing on the disintegration of Twain's family and his growing sense of rage at the world around him. An unbalanced but powerful book.

Kaplan, Justin. *Mr Clemens and Mark Twain.* New York: Simon & Schuster, 1970. A lively and well-written biography of Twain's most successful years (from 1866 on). Winner of the Pulitzer Prize for Biography and a benchmark for all biography since.

Powers, Ron. *Mark Twain: A Life.* New York: Simon & Schuster, 2005. The best of the full-life biographies written in recent years. Good use made of Twain's own correspondence, but pays little attention to Twain's last decade.

Steinbrink, Jeffrey. *Getting to Be Mark Twain.* Berkeley: University of California Press, 1991. Intriguing study of Twain's life and career in the years 1867–1871.

Bibliography

Tenney, Thomas A. *Mark Twain: A Reference Guide.* Boston: G. K. Hall, 1977. Supplements in the journals *American Literary Realism* and the *Mark Twain Circular.* For more recent bibliography, see the major Twain critical works and websites (below).

General reference guides

Camfield, Gregg. *The Oxford Companion to Mark Twain*. New York: Oxford
    University Press, 2003. Part-encyclopaedia, part-essay collection, an A-Z
    approach to key Twain subjects and texts. Oddball, but often penetrating.
Gribben, Alan. *Mark Twain's Library: A Reconstruction*. 2 vols. Boston: G.K. Hall,
    1980. Invaluable resource for tracing what Twain was reading and its
    influence on him.
LeMaster, J. R. and Wilson, James D. *The Mark Twain Encyclopedia*. New York:
    Garland Publishing, 1993. Useful series of (mostly short) essays on works,
    characters and Twain-related topics. Some unevenness in quality.
Rasmussen, R. Kent. *Mark Twain A–Z: The Essential Reference Guide to His Life
    and Writings*. New York: Oxford University Press, 1995. This book is what
    it says it is – essential. Contains general information about Twain and the
    thick context of his life and works (plots, people, places, and all related
    knowledge). Factual and avoids critical opinion.

Critical overviews of Twain (edited collections)

Bloom, Harold (ed.). *Mark Twain*. New York: Chelsea House Publishers, 1986. A
    well-balanced collection and wide-ranging introduction to Twain.
Budd, Louis J. (ed.). *Mark Twain: The Contemporary Reviews*. Cambridge:
    Cambridge University Press, 1999. Impressive collection of newspaper and
    journal responses to Twain's work in his lifetime.
Fishkin, Shelley Fisher. *A Historical Guide to Mark Twain*. New York: Oxford
    University Press, 2002. Good essays by major Twain critics on a series of
    topics including race, commerce, religion, gender, social class and
    imperialism
Messent, Peter and Budd, Louis J. (eds). *A Companion to Mark Twain*. Oxford:
    Blackwell, 2005. Substantive essay collection by noted Twain scholars.
    Sections include: cultural contexts, travel, publishing and performing, fiction
    and humour.
Robinson, Forrest (ed). *The Cambridge Companion to Mark Twain*. Cambridge:
    Cambridge University Press, 1995. Punchy and unusual set of essays in this
    reliable series.
Sundquist, Eric J. *Mark Twain: A Collection of Critical Essays*. Englewood Cliffs,
    N. J.: Prentice Hall, 1994. Excellent short collection, mostly on the major
    works.

Critical overviews of Twain (single-authored works)

Budd, Louis J. *Mark Twain: Social Philosopher*. Bloomington: Indiana Uniervsity
    Press, 1962. Comprehensive study of the development of Twain's social and
    political attitudes and relationship to his historical times.

Cox, James M. *Mark Twain: The Fate of Humor*. Princeton, N.J.: Princeton University Press, 1966. An important early book exploring Twain's use of humour and how it relates to the serious issues addressed in his work.

Knoper, Randall. *Acting Naturally: Mark Twain in the Culture of Performance*. Berkeley: University of California Press, 1995. Examines performance and the use of dramatic device in Twain, paying close attention to class, race, gender and economic and scientific change.

Lowry, Richard S. *'Littery Man': Mark Twain and Modern Authorship*. New York: Oxford University Press, 1996. On Twain, his career as a writer and publisher, and the professionalisation of literature in the US. Strong on Twain and realism.

Messent, Peter. *Mark Twain*. Houndmills: Macmillan, 1997. Introductory overview and close critical analysis of the major texts.

Michelson, Bruce. *Mark Twain on the Loose: A Comic Writer and the American Self*. Amherst: University of Massachusetts Press, 1995. Sparky and stimulating study exploring the outrageous and anarchic sides of Twain's humour and its cultural importance.

Smith, Henry Nash. *Mark Twain: The Development of a Writer*. Cambridge, Mass.: Harvard University Press, 1962. Another important early study, focusing on Twain's use of vernacular language and values and on 'the matter of Hannibal'.

Books about *Adventures of Huckleberry Finn*

Arac, Jonathan. *Huckleberry Finn as Idol and Target: The Functions of Criticism in Our Time*. Madison: University of Wisconsin Press, 1997. Contentious but important book, exploring Twain's novel in the context of American cultural history and interrogating its 'hypercanonization'.

Blair, Walter. *Mark Twain & Huck Finn*. Berkeley: University of California Press, 1962. On the factors – biographical, philosophical and artistic – contributing to the making of the novel. The account of the composition process is now outmoded, but still a valuable study.

Budd, Louis J. (ed.). *New Essays on Huckleberry Finn*. Cambridge: Cambridge University Press, 1985. Good short collection of essays in a reliable series.

Fishkin, Shelley Fisher. *Was Huck Black? Mark Twain and African-American Voices*. New York: Oxford University Press, 1993. Important argument about the way African American voices, language and rhetorical traditions figure in Twain's novel. An influential book.

Leonard, James S., Tenney, Thomas A., and Davis, Thadious M. (eds.). *Satire or Evasion? Black Perspectives on Huckleberry Finn*. Durham: Duke University Press, 1992. Collection of essays by African American scholars reassessing the racial aspects of the novel.

Sattelmeyer, Robert, and Crowley, J. Donald (eds.). *One Hundred Years of Huckleberry Finn: The Boy, His Book, and American Culture*. Columbia: University of Missouri Press, 1985. Substantial centenary collection of essays.

CD Rom on *Adventures of Huckleberry Finn*

*Huck Finn: The Complete Buffalo & Erie County Public Library Manuscript –
Teaching and Research Digital Edition*, 2003. Invaluable source and other
material collated by Victor Doyno. Contains Twain's manuscript version of
the novel and the alterations he made, plus a wealth of critical and
background information.

Books about *Puddn'head Wilson*

Robinson, Forrest G., and Gillman, Susan (eds.). *Mark Twain's Pudd'nhead
Wilson: Race, Conflict, and Culture.* Durham: Duke University Press, 1990.
Strong collection of essays.

The short works

Messent, Peter. *The Short Works of Mark Twain: A Critical Study.* Philadelphia:
University of Pennsylvania Press, 2001. A close study of the collections of
short writings Twain published in his lifetime.
Quirk, Tom. *Mark Twain: A Study of the Short Fiction.* New York: Twayne, 1997.
Good introductory study divided by period, plus a selection of critical essays
by others.

The travel books

Bridgman, Richard. *Traveling in Mark Twain.* Berkeley: University of California
Press, 1987. Sharp analysis of Twain's use of the travel book form and of the
travel narratives.
Melton, Jeffrey Alan. *Mark Twain, Travel Books, and Tourism: The Tide of a Great
Popular Movement.* Tuscaloosa: University of Alabama Press, 2002. How
Twain subverts generic expectations and how the travel books reflect his
intellectual and emotional growth.

Twain and gender

Harris, Susan K. *The Courtship of Olivia Langdon and Mark Twain.* Cambridge:
Cambridge University Press, 1996. A study of the courtship and gender roles
and of the intellectual and emotional life of the couple.
Stahl, J. D. *Mark Twain, Culture and Gender: Envisioning America through Europe.*
Athens: University of Georgia Press, 1994. Careful study of Twain's shifting

conceptions of gender and sexuality in his European fictional and non-fictional work.

Stoneley, Peter. *Mark Twain and the Feminine Aesthetic.* Cambridge: Cambridge University Press, 1992. An exploration of Twain's preoccupation with the role, nature and value of the 'feminine' over a wide range of his writings.

The late writings

Gillman, Susan. *Dark Twins: Imposture and Identity in Mark Twain's America.* Chicago: University of Chicago Press, 1989. Highly theorised but perceptive book on Twain and identity, his explorations of racial and sexual difference and the late Dream Writings.

Internet sites

Mark Twain (http://www.boondocksnet.com/twainwww/) Edited by Jim Zwick. Wide ranging site with especially good material on anti-imperialism.

Mark Twain at Large: His Travels Here and Abroad (http://www.lib.berkeley.edu/BANC/Exhibits/MTP/) From the Mark Twain Papers at Berkeley. An excellent exhibition on Twain's travel writing.

Mark Twain in His Times (http://etext.virginia.edu/railton/index2.html) From the University of Virginia. Invaluable site. Primary and secondary texts, contemporary reviews and articles, images, interactive exhibits.

www.twainquotes.com (http://www.twainquotes.com/quotesatoz.html) Very useful alphabetical subject-directory of Twain quotes, maxims and opinions.

Index